1000
James Bond
Facts

Tom Chapman

Other books by Tom Chapman:

1000 Serial Killer Facts
1000 World War 2 Facts

Contents

Introduction

Think you know all there is to know about James Bond? Well, think again. 1000 James Bond Facts contains all the trivia you could ever wish to know about this legendary hero of literature and the silver screen. Books, films, stunts, casting, Bond actors, music, behind the scenes, gadgets, Ian Fleming, what might have been, deleted scenes, Bond Girls, and much more.

So, park up the Lotus Esprit and Aston Martin, loosen that tuxedo, pour yourself a vodka martini, and prepare to enter the incredible and amazing world of James Bond...

Facts

(1) During World War 2, James Bond author Ian Fleming was in charge of 30 Assault Unit - a commando force that was deployed behind German lines. Fleming also advised the United States on setting up the OSS, the precursor to the CIA. By the end of the war, Ian Fleming was a Commander - just like James Bond.

(2) In the PTS of 1981's For Your Eyes Only, most people are baffled when the ersatz Blofeld (impaled on Bond's helicopter) says - "I'll buy you delicatessen in stainless steel!" This line was suggested by Cubby Broccoli. Apparently it was an old saying that New York mob people would say when they wanted to negotiate or do business. The writers on the film hated the delicatessen line but Cubby was the boss so it ended up in the movie.

(3) In early plans for the film adaptation of On Her Majesty's Secret Service, Blofeld's headquarters was going to be located on the Maginot Line.

The Maginot Line was a series of fortifications built by the French in the 1930s to protect themselves from any German aggression. It was manned by the French army and even had its own subway system. It proved to be ineffective in World War 2 because the Germans aimed the focal point of their attack at the Ardennes region of Belgium and simply bypassed the Maginot Line. After the war ended, French troops were stationed at the Maginot Line again and one of its biggest bunkers became a NATO command centre. When France left NATO in 1966, the Maginot Line was abandoned.

(4) Roger Moore said that when he played James Bond he used to pretend the villain had halitosis in order to make himself appear somewhat repulsed whenever Bond encountered the baddie.

(5) The James Bond books were turned into a movie franchise in 1962 by New York born film producer Albert 'Cubby' Broccoli and Canadian producer Harry Saltzman. "Harry Saltzman held the option on Ian Fleming's James Bond stories," said Broccoli, "and I offered him a partnership. He considered them a bit of nonsense. I thought they offered all the basics in screen entertainment: a virile and resourceful hero, exotic locations, the ingenious apparatus of espionage and sex on a sophisticated level. It's true they had been around for a long time, and none of the leading British and American producers had made a serious pitch for them."

(6) There had been many film franchises before Bond - like Tarzan, Sherlock Holmes, Charlie Chan, The Falcon, Jungle Jim, Frankenstein, Lassie, Rin Tin Tin, Bulldog Drummond, Hopalong Cassidy, and many others. The James Bond franchise created by producers Cubby Broccoli and Harry Saltzman however was revolutionary. Previous film series operated strictly on the law of diminishing returns and lowered the budgets on each sequel accordingly. They sought to extract every last penny out of their licenced property without actually spending any money. The Bond series reversed this tradition. Each new Bond film was bigger than the one that came before. More lavish, more expensive, and more spectacular.

(7) On the first day of shooting for On Her Majesty's Secret Service, a security guard on the gate at Pinewood Studios didn't recognise George Lazenby and wouldn't let him in.

(8) In 1967, Sean Connery's brother Neil starred in an Italian James Bond knock-off film called O.K. Connery (aka Operation Kid Brother). A large number of familiar faces from the Bond films appeared in the movie with Neil Connery - including Bernard Lee, Lois Maxwell, Adolfo Celi, and Daniela Bianchi.

Neil Connery looked a little bit like Sean but had none of his brother's charisma or screen presence. Neil was dubbed in the film because he had a medical condition involving his throat at the time and couldn't speak very well. O.K. Connery is terrible film objectively but could be seen as a guilty pleasure. Lois Maxwell said that Sean Connery was very angry that Bond regulars had agreed to appear in the Italian movie and felt betrayed by them. The ironic thing is that Lois Maxwell was better paid on O.K. Connery than she ever was on the Bond movies!

(9) James Bond's famous request that his vodka martini be shaken and not stirred came from a theory Ian Fleming had that stirring alcoholic drinks somehow impaired the taste of them.

(10) Caroline Bliss was still only in her twenties when she made The Living Daylights and remains the only Moneypenny actress to play the part in spectacles. In a strange quirk of fate, Caroline Bliss was a childhood friend of Samantha Bond - who replaced her as Moneypenny for the Pierce Brosnan films in the 1990s.

(11) The James Bond series did invent the big budget action franchise but even Cubby Broccoli and Harry Saltzman had their own influences in 1962. The Bond series was heavily influenced by Alfred Hitchcock's masterful 1959 suspense thriller North By Northwest.

North By Northwest was in many ways the first James Bond film. It has a suave leading man, adventure, action, varied locations, panache, urbane villains, suggestive humour. The helicopter sequence in From Russia With Love is clearly inspired the crop dusting sequence in North By Northwest.

(12) The Bond producers were so inspired by North By Northwest that they even tried to persuade Cary Grant (who was a friend of Cubby Broccoli) to play James Bond in Dr No. Grant, who was in his early sixties at the time, declined this offer though because he felt he was far too old for the part.

(13) The James Bond movie franchise has tended to cherrypick titles, character names, and scenes from the Fleming books rather than adapt them wholesale. To give an example, the 1979 film Moonraker has little to do with Ian Fleming's 1955 novel of the same name - aside from the villain having the name Hugo Drax. The movie is about a villain who wants to create a new utopia in space whereas the book is about a secret government missile project on the Kent coast that James Bond has to investigate.

(14) The one Bond movie that did get a fairly faithful (to Fleming) adaptation is 1969's On Her Majesty's Secret Service. This is one of the reasons why that film is so highly regarded amongst Bond fans.

(15) 1989's Licence To Kill was the first Bond movie not to have a Fleming title.

(16) Although the first Bond came out in 1962, James Bond nearly hit the big screen much sooner. Before the birth of the James Bond franchise by Cubby Broccoli and Harry Saltzman, the Irish producer Kevin McClory had worked with Ian Fleming in the late 1950s on plans for what would have been the first movie featuring James Bond.

The screenplay for this proposed Bond film was called Longitude 78 West and also James Bond of the Secret Serivice. Fleming (rather foolishly) later used Longitude 78 West as the basis for his novel Thunderball. All hell broke loose because Fleming didn't give McClory or Jack Whittingham (who had also worked on Longitude 78 West) any credit. The inevitable court case which followed left Kevin McClory with the legal right to make a James Bond film based on Thunderball.

(17) Cubby Broccoli was very shrewd in the way that he handled Kevin McClory. He brought McClory in as a co-producer on EON's 1965 film version of Thunderball and made McClory agree not to produce a Thunderball film of his own

for at least ten years. Broccoli probably presumed (not unreasonably) the James Bond series wouldn't even be around in ten years time. Once the ten years were up though, the Bond series was still around and Kevin McClory set about making his own Bond film. McClory's plans to make a Bond film in the seventies called Warhead were frustrated but his long threatened and unofficial renegade Bond film finally arrived in 1983 with Never Say Never Again.

(18) The original title of the 1989 film Licence To Kill was License Revoked. The title was changed because market research indicated that American audiences associated the word revoked with driving licences.

(19) In the 1955 novel Moonraker we learn that James Bond is paid a salary of £1,500 a year. That would equate to around £40,000 in today's money.

(20) Ian Fleming's most experimental James Bond novel was The Spy Who Loved Me in 1962. This story is told first person by Vivienne Michel. Vivienne is closing down an empty hotel in the mountainous Adirondacks when two hoodlums turn up with orders to set the hotel on fire for the insurance. Vivienne is obviously someone these hoodlums need to eliminate to achieve their plan. She is saved though by the arrival of a mysterious stranger named James Bond.

Fleming's The Spy Who Loved Me has almost nothing to do with the 1977 Roger Moore film of the same name. Fleming was unhappy with the book and stipulated that only the title could be used. One thing that does influence the movie though is Fleming's character Sol "Horror" Horowitz. Horowitz is a villain with steel-capped teeth. He was clearly the inspiration for Richard Kiel's Jaws in the 1977 movie.

(21) Before he became a film producer, Cubby Broccoli had a spell selling coffins. He was also a Christmas tree salesman at one point.

(22) The James Bond series used to be the biggest grossing movie franchise of all time. It now ranks fifth behind Marvel, Star Wars, Harry Potter, and Spider-Man.

(23) Ian Fleming's James Bond books were very popular because their blend of sex, sadism, and adventure felt like something new and even risque at the time. British readers loved the James Bond books in the 1950s because the exotic nature of the novels was an escape from the lingering post-war austerity they still experienced.

(24) The literary Bond suffers from "accidie" - this is Fleming's definition of boredom and the deadliest of all sins for James Bond.

(25) If the film treatment for Longitude 78 West had become the first ever Bond film in the late 1950s, memos from Ian Fleming indicate that he liked the idea of Richard Burton playing 007 in the film. Burton however was apparently not interested in the vague approaches concerning this (ultimately doomed) project.

(26) Felix Leiter was named after a friend of Ian Fleming named John Leiter.

(27) In the Fleming novels, OO agents must retire from active service at the age of 45. James Bond doesn't expect to live this long anyway.

(28) Around the time that Thunderball (which was peak Bondmania for the Bond franchise) was released, Sean Connery received about 1,500 fan letters a week.

(29) In the books, James Bond gained his OO status by killing a Japanese cypher agent in New York.

(30) Adjusted for inflation, the most financially successful James Bond film of all time is 1965's Thunderball.

(31) James Bond's jet pack in Thunderball was a real prototype developed by the American military.

(32) Ian Fleming was a consultant on The Man From U.N.C.L.E. television spy action series from 1962 to 1963. Cubby Broccoli complained that Fleming was helping the opposition!

(33) The actor Richard Johnson was offered the part of James Bond in Dr No but he declined the part because he didn't like the idea of being under a long term contract. The odd thing about Johnson is that he later appeared in a host of forgotten James Bond imitation films. "I was under contract to MGM anyway, so that gave me a reasonable excuse to say no, because they told me I'd have to be under exclusive contract to them for seven years," said Johnson. "Eventually they offered it to Sean Connery, who was completely wrong for the part. But in getting the wrong man they got the right man, because it turned the thing on its head and he made it funny. And that's what propelled it to success."

(34) The acronym of SPECTRE stands for Special Executive for Counter-intelligence, Terrorism, Revenge, Extortion.

(35) One interesting thing they used to do in Bond films that connected the actors was to reference the death of Bond's wife Tracy in On Her Majesty's Secret Service. Roger Moore's Bond is noticeably touchy in The Spy Who Loved Me when Barbara Bach as Anya Amasova mentions that he was once married. The PTS of For Your Eyes Only begins with Roger's Bond placing flowers on the grave of his wife. This scene was actually written for a new Bond actor because they didn't think Roger was coming back. It was left in though and provides a nice little 'human' moment for Roger's Bond.

In 1989's Licence To Kill, Timothy Dalton smiles weakly and refuses to accept a garter from Della when she tells him that he'll be the next to get married. These little moments in the Moore and Dalton films were a nice touch and connected the cinematic Bonds in a very understated but effective way. By the time of the Brosnan and Craig films, the references to Bond's wife were dropped. Too much time had passed.

(36) Ian Fleming got the name for his famous hero from a book called Field Guide to the Birds of the West Indies. The author of this book was a man named James Bond.

(37) In the film Diamonds Are Forever, Bond has membership of the Playboy Club. His membership number is 40401.

(38) The German actor Gert Frobe had to be dubbed as Auric Goldfinger because when he spoke English no one could understand a word he was saying.

(39) Jane Seymour suffered a bout of dysentery shooting Live and Let Die in Jamaica.

(40) In the film Dr No, Bond is an MI7 agent. There is on such thing as MI7 in either the Fleming books or real life.

(41) Ian Fleming wrote Casino Royale on a gold-plated typewriter. In 1995, Fleming's typewriter was auctioned at Christie's for £50,000.

(42) Fleming's original title for Live and Let Die was The Undertaker's Wind.

(43) The profile of the Bond novels got a huge boost when President John F. Kennedy named From Russia With Love as one of his books of the year.

(44) Ian Fleming initially hated the choice of Sean Connery to play James Bond. Fleming thought that Connery was too rough and not refined enough to play his hero. However, Fleming changed his mind when he saw Connery in action. The suave director Terence Young played a big role in the transformation of Connery. Young had his tailor cut sharp suits for Connery and taught him how to be more elegant and

refined onscreen.

(45) Ian Fleming's literary Bond became an orphan at the age of eleven when his parents died in a climbing accident.

(46) The grand tradition of the PTS (pre-title sequence) featuring a spectacular stunt involving James Bond was only really established in 1977's The Spy Who Loved Me when Bond memorably skied off a mountain ledge in a banana yellow ski-suit to evade various gun toting goons. After that it was expected (and hugely anticipated) that each Bond film would begin with a jawdropping stunt sequence. Before the tradition established by The Spy Who loved Me, the pre-title sequences were a little more experimental and unpredictable. Sure, sometimes you got Bond involved in stunts and action (like Goldfinger and Thunderball) but they also had more licence to do something slightly strange or moody.

(47) When Goldfinger came out, there was an urban legend that Shirley Eaton had died as a result of being covered in gold paint. In reality, Shirley Eaton was (and still is) very much alive and you can't actually die from painting your skin.

(48) In the legendary sequence in Goldfinger where Bond is strapped to a table as Auric Goldfinger demonstrates his laser, there was someone under the table with a blowtorch to give the effect of the laser cutting into the surface. It was an understandably nervous experience for Sean Connery.

(49) An incredible 600 women were considered for the part of Domino in Thunderball. There were around 150 auditions in the end.

(50) In the Ian Fleming books, James Bond has a particular dislike for short people and mustaches! His ultimate nightmare would presumably be a short person with a large mustache.

(51) For the scenes in Goldeneye where Bond and Onatopp

suggestively wrestle in the sauna, the tiles on the wall were made of rubber and foam so that Pierce Brosnan and Famke Janssen couldn't get hurt. Janssen did actually get slightly hurt in the end though when they got carried away.

(52) No Time To Die was very nearly called A Reason To Die. The night before the press conference for the start of shooting, the studio and producers got cold feet about calling the film A Reason To Die though and scrapped the whole idea at the last minute. A Reason to Live, A Reason to Die was the name of a 1972 Spaghetti Western starring James Coburn and Telly Savalas.

(53) The Aston Martin was written into Goldfinger after Ian Fleming was loaned one of the cars to drive. The Aston Martin in the book was considerably less gadget festooned than the car in the Goldfinger movie.

(54) Brosnan's Bond is estimated to have killed 47 people in Goldeneye. That's a very hefty kill count for a Bond film.

(55) Ian Fleming lived long enough to see Dr No and From Russia With Love made into movies but - sadly - he died just before the release of Goldfinger. Fleming therefore never quite got to experience the peak Bondmania that his famous character created in the 1960s with Goldfinger and Thunderball.

(56) A lengthy sequence in On Her Majesty's Secret Service where Bond chases one of Blofeld's men over London rooftops was cut from the movie. George Lazenby must have been irritated to see this sequence hit the cutting room floor because he injured his arm shooting it.

(57) When he was cast as James Bond, Sean Connery worked with a dance teacher named Yat Malmgren so he could learn how to be more graceful and panther like in his movements and gestures.

(58) Seventeen boats were destroyed in the stunt rehearsals for Live and Let Die.

(59) The French premiere of Goldeneye was cancelled after Pierce Brosnan protested against French nuclear testing.

(60) When the Bond movie franchise began, Ian Fleming was allowed to sit in on production meetings and had final script approval.

(61) The costume department wanted to put Bond in pastel colours and designer clothes in Licence To Kill but Timothy Dalton didn't like this plan and wanted to wear plainer clothes in the film. Dalton argued that Bond was a spy who had gone rogue so should wear clothes that didn't make him stand out!

(62) The secret service in the Fleming books operate from a building which overlooks Regent's Park.

(63) Ian Fleming wrote many of the Bond books at his GoldenEye retreat in Jamaica.

(64) It was very chilly at Pinewood Studios when they shot some of the bedroom scenes for Bond and Solitare in Live and Let Die so Roger Moore and Jane Seymour wore football socks in bed to stay warm.

(65) Goldfinger was so popular that its soundtrack knocked the Beatles off the top of the American albums chart.

(66) When he became James Bond, Timothy Dalton was at pains to distance James Bond from contemporary action movie rivals like Rambo and Schwarzenegger. Dalton said that James Bond used ingenuity rather than brawn and wouldn't be seen dead pumping iron in a gym.

(67) In the Fleming books, Bond actually drinks more Scotch with soda than Martinis.

(68) Fleming's literary Bond is six feet tall in height.

(69) When Pierce Brosnan first had to drive the Aston Martin in Goldeneye, he left the handbrake on by mistake and damaged the car.

(70) On why he chose the name James Bond for her hero, Ian Fleming said - "It struck me that this brief, unromantic, Anglo-Saxon and yet very masculine name was just what I needed and so a second James Bond was born."

(71) Putter Smith, who plays the killer Mr Wint in Diamonds Are Forever, was a musician with no previous acting experience.

(72) Sales of Fleming's first Bond novel Casino Royale were poor at first. It took a while for the Bond books to become popular.

(73) Pierce Brosnan's Bond never visited the United States in any of his four films.

(74) Daniel Craig was the first Bond actor who wasn't born before the movie franchise began.

(75) Demand for Thunderball was so great that they had two simultaneous premieres in London full of celebrities, glitz, and huge crowds of fans. Sean Connery never turned up to either of them.

(76) When they were shooting The Spy Who Loved Me in Egypt, the Egyptian government assigned an official to the production whose job it was to make that nothing in the movie or script was at all derogatory about Egypt. Bond's wisecrack in the film about "Egyptian builders" was therefore dubbed in much later in the safety of Pinewood Studios thousands of miles away.

(77) In the novel On Her Majesty's Secret Service, we learn

that Bond visits the grave of Vesper Lynd (from Casino Royale) once a year.

(78) Krystyna Skarbek, an agent Ian Fleming met during the war, was the inspiration for Vesper Lynd.

(79) The biggest difference between the James Bond books written by Ian Fleming and the James Bond film franchise created by Cubby Broccoli and Harry Saltzman was humour. The films gave Bond (played by the peerless Sean Connery) deadpan quips and witty lines. Humour became an essential part of the franchise.

(80) Sean Connery quickly tired of the fame and attention afforded to him by Bondmania in the 1960s. Connery called James Bond his Frankenstein's Monster. One of the reasons why Connery left the franchise in 1967 (though he did return in 1971) was that he felt it was constrictive playing the same character all the time. He wanted to embrace new challenges as an actor and get away from his Bond image.

(81) The absolute apex of Sean Connery's annoyance with all things 007 is said to have famously arrived when a photographer tried to follow him into the toilet and take his picture while he was shooting You Only Live Twice.

(82) Roger Moore never drove Bond's trademark Aston Martin in any of his films. Roger's Bond drove a Lotus instead.

(83) The Bond films started using the real life MI6 building at Vauxhall from Goldeneye onwards. Before this, Bond had his briefings at offices on Whitehall (in the Roger Moore films) and Trafalgar Square and the Mall (in the Dalton films).

(84) Jane Seymour was only twenty years old when she was cast as Solitare in Live and Let Die.

(85) Ricou Browning, the director of underwater photography on Thunderball, was the man in the monster suit in the classic

horror film Creature from the Black Lagoon.

(86) In 2013, Joan Collins revealed that she turned down the part of Jill Masterson in Goldfinger. "I was asked to do the Shirley Eaton part in the Sean Connery Bond film Goldfinger - the classic role in which she is naked and sprayed from head to foot in gold paint. It's an amazing image and an amazing film but I turned it down. I was pregnant at the time with my son Sacha. Who knows? It could have altered the direction of my whole career and I sometimes wonder what would have happened if I had done it. I have never talked about it before and it's not in my new book because I didn't want to be bitchy to Shirley."

(87) James Bond's car in Thunderball is capable of projecting high pressure jets of water. This effect was achieved in a fairly simple way. They simply ran the hose from an unseen fire engine through the Aston Martin.

(88) There are any number of reasons why Sean Connery tired of playing James Bond. For one, he felt like he had no privacy anymore. Wherever he went he was besiged by fans. Connery couldn't even go out for a quiet meal without being asked for an autograph (his annoyance was frequently made worse by people asking him to sign autographs James Bond rather than Sean Connery). Connery was also frustrated that the Bond films became increasingly elaborate and lengthy productions because this made it more difficult for him to find the time to play other more rewarding (from his point of view) roles.

Another reason why Connery became embittered was money. Broccoli and Saltzman were raking it in with the Bond franchise in the 1960s and Connery felt he should have been made a partner and given a more generous share of the profits. "It's not that I needed the money," said Connery in 1971, "I'm a relatively wealthy man. It was the fact that I put in an awful lot of work and energy into the Bond pictures and was not sufficiently rewarded. The producers were getting greedy. I had an awful time getting the money out of them." In mitigation, Broccoli and Saltzman might have argued that they were the ones who made Connery a film star in the first place. Sean Connery would have been nowhere near as rich and famous without James Bond.

(89) Ian Fleming once wrote that the James Bond books were written for 'for warm-blooded heterosexuals in railway trains, airplanes and beds'.

(90) Sean Connery said he enjoyed making the first Bond films but it became a drag in the end. "The first two or three were fun. The cast made it fun. Jumping out of planes was entertaining although it was tough on my hair piece. It eventually became too dominant in everything I was doing. There was no way to compete with it and try to get any justifiable balance."

(91) Daniel Craig said that the first Bond film he ever watched as a child was Live and Let Die.

(92) Martine Beswick, who had small parts in From Russia with Love and Thunderball, was one of the dancing girls in the title sequence for Dr No.

(93) In an early draft of the Diamonds Are Forever script, Bond's final battle with Wint and Kidd took place in the lower decks of the ship.

(94) In the Ian Fleming Bond novels, SPECTRE have been in operation since 1956.

(95) In the original script for Dr No, writer Richard Maibaum had a villain named Buchfield and Dr No was merely the name of Buchfield's monkey. Cubby Broccoli thought this was complete nonsense and canned the script. Needless to say, Maibaum was ribbed about his Dr No monkey idea for years to come by the Bond people.

(96) Daniel Craig's main competition for the part of James

Bond in Casino Royale, once the long list of potential actors had been whittled down by numerous interviews, readings, auditions, and screen tests, was a fairly unknown young English born Australian actor named Sam Worthington and a completely unknown 22 year-old actor from the Channel Islands named Henry Cavill. Sam Worthington and Henry Cavill were later both very successful in their own right after their unsuccessful brush with potential Bond fame. Worthington starred in big films like Avatar and Terminator Salvation while Cavill became Superman.

(97) Blofeld made his first movie appearance in From Russia with Love. We do not see his face though. The voice of Blofeld was supplied by Eric Pohlmann.

(98) Bond was essentially the first action franchise. It invented a whole new genre. Without the James Bond franchise there would have been no Indiana Jones, no Jason Bourne, no Derek Flint, and no Ethan Hunt. Everyone from Steven Spielberg to James Cameron to Christopher Nolan was hugely influenced by the Bond films.

(99) Raquel Welch originally signed to play Domino in Thunderball but Broccoli and Saltzman gave her permission to leave the production and make Fantastic Voyage for 20th Century Fox.

(100) Tula, one of the girls at the swimming pool in for Your Eyes Only, was born Barry Cossey. After a sex-change operation, she became a model.

(101) Thunderball was so popular in Britain that some cinemas sold all their seats and then sold extra tickets to customers who were willing to stand!

(102) In the film Live and Let Die, Bond is told that "Hamilton" has been killed in New York. This is a joke based on the fact that Guy Hamilton directed the film.

(103) Licence To Kill is fairly light on gadgets but there are some decent ones all the same. Bond fans will be well aware that Bond's signature gun (the optical palm reader means that the firing mechanism will only respond to 007's grip) is an idea that was later 'borrowed' (stolen might be a better word) for the Sam Mendes Bond film Spectre.

(104) Stuntman Wayne Michaels did the bungee jump which begins Goldeneye. He plunged from a height of 720 feet.

(105) Cubby Broccoli told George Lazenby not to come to the On Her Majesty's Secret Service premiere looking scruffy. You can probably guess what happened. Lazenby, ever the rebel, turned up with long hair and a beard!

(106) Lois Chiles turned down the part of Anya Amasova in The Spy Who Loved Me. Chiles did though accept the role of Holly Goodhead in the next Bond film Moonraker.

(107) Timothy Dalton started shooting The Living Daylights only one day after finishing work on a Brooke Shields film called Brenda Starr.

(108) The Goldeneye tank chase in St Petersburg was finished on replica streets at the studio at Leavesden. At one point the tank went out of control and crushed a panavision camera.

(109) Live and Let Die was called The Dead Slave in Japan.

(110) Charles Gray played Blofeld in Diamonds Are Forever despite playing Henderson in You Only Live Twice only a few films previously. Gray is a very urbane and civilised Blofeld and nothing like past Blofeld actors.

(111) When he became Bond in 1972, Roger Moore signed a three film contract. After he completed this deal with The Spy Who Loved Me, Roger's subsequent appearances as Bond were negotiated on a film by film basis.

(112) Harry Saltzman left the Bond franchise in 1974 after The Man with the Golden Gun. He sold his 50% stake in James Bond to United Artists. Cubby Broccoli retained the other 50% and became the solo producer on the Bond movies from The Spy Who Loved Me onwards.

(113) The US army jet pack in Thunderball required two pilots to be on the set as they were the only people trained to fly it.

(114) One of the red 1969 Mercury Cougar XR-7s driven by Diana Rigg in On Her Majesty's Secret Service sold at Bonhams auction house in 2020 for £356,500.

(115) In the Fleming novels, Bond has a Scottish housekeeper called May. This character was not translated into the movies. The reason why May is not a character in the movies is mostly because we rarely see Bond at home during the films and having a housekeeper seems a rather bygone old-fashioned type of thing.

(116) Some real police officers were used as extras in the speedboat chases in Live and Let Die.

(117) Paulina Porizkova and Eva Herzigova were considered for the part of Natalya in Goldeneye.

(118) One of the reasons why Judi Dench was cast as M (besides being a great actress) is that it was revealed in 1993 that the real life head of MI5 was a woman Stella Rimington. MI5 is the United Kingdom's domestic counter-intelligence and security agency and part of its intelligence machinery alongside the Secret Intelligence Service (MI6).

(119) Fleming's Bond is the son of a Scottish father, Andrew Bond and a Swiss mother, Monique Delacroix.

(120) One of the original plans for the film Diamonds Are Forever was for the villain to be Goldfinger's twin brother. Gert Frobe was even approached before this idea was

abandoned.

(121) The villain Franz Sanchez in Licence To Kill is based on Colombian drug lord and narcoterrorist Pablo Escobar.

(122) The SMERSH dossier on James Bond in Fleming's From Russia with Love is as follows - 'First name: JAMES. Height: 183 centimeters; weight: 76 kilograms; slim build; eyes: blue; hair: black; scar down right cheek and on left shoulder; signs of plastic surgery on back of right hand (see Appendix A); all-round athlete; expert pistol shot, boxer, knife-thrower; does not use disguises. Languages: French and German. Smokes heavily (N.B.: special cigarettes with three gold bands); vices: drink, but not to excess, and women. Not thought to accept bribes. This man is invariably armed with a .25 Beretta automatic carried in a holster under his left arm. Magazine holds eight rounds. Has been known to carry a knife strapped to his left forearm; has used steel capped shoes; knows the basic holds of judo. In general, fights with tenacity and has a high tolerance of pain (see Appendix B).'

(123) The original theme song for Thunderball was Mr Kiss Kiss Bang Bang (the Italian nickname for Bond). This song was recorded by both Shirley Bassey and Dionne Warick. United Artists did not like the fact though that the song didn't mention the movie's title and so at the last minute a new song (Thunderball by Tom Jones) replaced Mr Kiss Kiss Bang Bang. United Artists might have regretted that decision in the end because Thunderball by Tom Jones didn't sell especially well - at least in comparison to Goldfinger.

(124) Fleming's Dr No novel has a passage where James Bond grapples with a giant squid. It's probably no surprise that this sequence has never been adapted in any of the movies.

(125) As part of the deal with Ian Fleming to bring James Bond to the big screen, it was agreed that EON would have permission to write original Bond films if they exhausted the Fleming stories. This was obviously a shrewd agreement on

the part of the film producers.

(126) Dr No has Goya's portrait of the Duke of Wellington in his art collection. This portrait had been stolen in real life when Dr No went into production.

(127) George Lazenby was up against John Richardson, Hans de Vries, Robert Campbell and Anthony Rogers in the final James Bond auditions for On Her Majesty's Secret Service.

(128) Roger Moore said in his memoir that although people tend to think of For Your Eyes Only as more grounded and serious than his other films he didn't notice any departure in tone or style when he was actually making the film.

(129) It is obviously somewhat awkward today that the Afghan freedom fighters in The Living Daylights are the people who became the Taliban!

(130) James Bond drives a Bentley in the Fleming novels. This car appeared in the film From Russia With Love.

(131) In the Fleming books, both Auric Goldfinger and Hugo Drax cheat at cards. In the refined world of Ian Fleming this is obviously a warning sign that someone is a villain and not a gentleman in the least!

(132) George Lazenby said he only got the part of James Bond about two weeks before shooting was due to commence for On Her Majesty's Secret Service.

(133) The company set up by Cubby Broccoli and Harry Saltzman to produce the Bond films is called EON. EON means Everything or Nothing.

(134) Sean Connery was largely unknown when he was cast as James Bond in Dr No. Cubby Broccoli's wife Dana had suggested Connery after watching him in a Disney film called Darby O'Gill and the Little People.

(135) In the 1983 television movie Return of the Man from U.N.C.L.E., George Lazenby has a cameo as tuxedo clad agent who drives an Aston Martin with number plate JB 007.

(136) For the production of Thunderball, a full size mock-up of a Vulcan bomber was constructed with fibreglass and then sunk.

(137) The news that George Lazenby had probably quit Bond franchise leaked before On Her Majesty's Secret Service was released. As a consequence, the promotional campaign downplayed Lazenby and billed James Bond as the star. This was very different from the Connery films - which also made a big deal od declaring that Sean Connery IS James Bond.

(138) In Thunderball, all the 00 agents are required to attend a meeting. There are nine seats - indicating that there are nine agents in the OO section.

(139) Jaws was originally going to be killed in an inferno in The Spy Who Loved Me but the Bond team were shrewd enough to sense the potential of the character and so shot an alternative ending in which he survived.

(140) The 2006 film Casino Royale is the first Bond movie to have a black and white sequence.

(141) At a 2014 auction, one of Bond's safari shirts from The Man with the Golden Gun fetched nearly £5,000.

(142) Bond's code number '007' was apparently inspired by a bus route in Kent which was often taken by the author Ian Fleming.

(143) The advantage Bond films had over other franchises was to always set themselves in the present day - or 'five minutes into the future' as Cubby Broccoli liked to say. You basically get the same film but dressed up in new fashions and

technology. It's a formula that has worked surprisingly well.

(144) In Ian Fleming's Casino Royale novel, Bond played baccarat against Le Chiffre. This was changed to poker in the 2006 film.

(145) John Landis claims that Cubby Broccoli offered him the chance to direct 1989's Licence To Kill and said he declined because he was used to have final cut on his movies.

(146) It was decided when Roger Moore became Bond not to immediately saddle him with too many of the iconic 007 trappings associated with Sean Connery. It took three films, for example, before we saw Roger in a naval commander uniform. The initial reluctance to invite comparisons between Moore and Connery was shrewd and helped Roger Moore to make the part his own.

(147) Peter Hunt, the editor on the early Bond films, said they only realised what a sensation they had on their hands when they screened Dr No for an audience. Before that, they genuinely didn't know if audiences would like Dr No or not.

(149) Michael Kitchen did not reprise his role as Tanner in Tomorrow Never Dies becase he was too busy. The character of Robinson played by Colin Salmon sort of replaced him but then both Tanner and Robinson appeared in Brosnan's third film The World is Not enough.

(150) Jack Lord was the first person to play Felix Leiter (in Dr No). The Bond screenwriter Richard Maibaum said Lord didn't return because he demanded equal billing with Sean Connery and a much bigger fee for the next picture. Jack Lord didn't seem to realise that these were James Bond movies - not James Bond & Felix Leiter movies!

(151) Timothy Dalton was the last James Bond who was briefed through those leather padded doors at Universal Exports rather than the MI6 building at Vauxhall Cross.

(152) Sean Connery couldn't attend the British premiere of Goldfinger because he was shooting The Hill in Spain.

(153) Guy Hamilton said that when he made Diamonds Are Forever there was a penalty clause in his contract that would be activated if he delivered a film over two hours long. They wanted the film under two hours in duration so that cinemas could fit in as many screenings as possible.

(154) An incredible 23 million people watched Live and Let Die when it was first broadcast on British television in 1980.

(155) Michael Billington, who was waiting in the wings to take over as James Bond in For Your Eyes Only and Octopussy if negotiations with Roger Moore broke down, later said that when he saw Roger dressed as a circus clown in Octopussy he was rather relieved he hadn't become 007.

(156) Willard Whyte in Diamonds Are Forever was inspired by Cubby Broccoli's reclusive friend Howard Hughes.

(157) There was no official press conference to unveil Timothy Dalton as Bond. This was a contrast to Pierce Brosnan in 1994 and Daniel Craig in 2005. These days you simply can't imagine them casting a new James Bond actor without arranging a fancy press conference to unveil him. Bond fans (and the media) would feel cheated if this didn't happen. Dalton simply went straight into shooting the film. The press only got to meet Timothy Dalton when a small press conference was held during the Daylights shoot in Vienna on October the 5th 1986.

(158) Four different Aston Martin cars were used in the production of Goldfinger.

(159) Ian Fleming considered calling his Moonraker novel The Infernal Machine.

(160) Roger Moore said he was first approached to play James

Bond in the late 1960s. Cubby and Harry were thinking about making The Man with the Golden Gun at the time. "At that time they were talking about going to Cambodia," said Roger, "and all hell broke loose and things got postponed. Lew Grade decided to sell a series Tony Curtis and I did - The Persuaders - which sort of precluded me from doing Bond. Then they had the search and came up with George Lazenby."

(161) Live and Let Die was one of the few Bond films that Richard Maibaum didn't write on. He was later critical of the movie. "To process drugs in the middle of the jungle is not a Bond caper," said Maibaum.

(162) One of the cast members of For Your Eyes Only was the Australian actress Cassandra Harris as Countess Lisl von Schlaf. Harris had recently got married to a young Irish actor named Pierce Brosnan. At the time, Brosnan's credits only amounted to small roles in The Long Good Friday and The Mirror Crack'd. During the production of the film, Cassandra Harris introduced Brosnan to Cubby Broccoli and Broccoli immediately made a mental note of Brosnan as a potential future Bond.

(163) The sadistic torture of Bond by Le Chiffre in Casino Royale was based on the French-Moroccan torture known as passer á la mandoline. Ian Fleming said this was actually done on captured Allied agents during the war.

(164) The weather in Jamaica was quite bad when they made Dr No and they couldn't shoot half the scenes they'd planned.

(165) When they began pre-production on For Your Eyes Only it was deemed very unlikely that Roger Moore would be back so they hired stuntmen with black hair because the favourites to become the new Bond were dark haired actors like James Brolin and Michael Billington. When they learned that Roger was coming back they had to get all their fair haired stuntmen back!

(166) Despite the media interest in the new James Bond actor in 1987, the press found Timothy Dalton a difficult person to write about because his private life was a complete mystery. Dalton had no interest at all in being a celebrity and was notoriously protective of his privacy. He rarely spoke about anything except acting. The press found it difficult to get much of an impression on Dalton as a person because he was basically invisible unless obliged to promote a film.

(167) The Eagle's nest was built for Hitler at Obersalzberg by Martin Bormann. This retreat was 6,000 feet up and built on the inside of a mountain. Hitler made some of his biggest decisions at the Eagle's Nest. The Alpine mountain complex of Blofeld in the James Bond film On Her Majesty's Secret Service was based on the Eagle's Nest.

(168) Victor Tourjansky was the bemused onlooker in three Roger Moore films. Tourjansky was the man with the bottle on the beach when the Lotus comes out the water in The Spy Who Loved Me, the man with bttle (again) in Moonraker, and then the man with the wine glass surprised by the ski chase in For Your Eyes Only. Tourjansky was an Italian born second assistant director and writer. You can only really imagine these comic cameos happening in the Roger Moore era.

(169) On the audio commentary for The Man with the Golden gun, Roger Moore said he didn't like the moment where Bond pushes the kid in the water.

(170) Gemma Arterton later said she regretted taking the part of Strawberry Fields in Quantum of Solace. "I still get criticism for accepting Quantum of Solace, but I was 21, I had a student loan, and you know, it was a Bond film. But as I got older I realised there was so much wrong with Bond women. Strawberry should have just said no [to having sex with Bond], really, and worn flat shoes."

(171) Casino Royale director Martin Campbell was brutally honest when he was asked what he thought of Marc Forster's

follow-up movie Quantum of Solace. "Oh, I thought it was lousy," said Campbell. "I just thought the story was pretty uninteresting. I didn't think the action was related to the characters. I just thought overall it was a bit of a mess really."

(172) The eighties Bond films had increasingly static budgets because they were still paying off the interest on Moonraker going over budget. John Glen complained that the static budgets of the Bond films at this time made it difficult to stage all the action in Licence To Kill.

(173) On Her Majesty's Secret Service was called 007 Seized The Snow Mountain Castle in Norway.

(174) When Timothy Dalton asked about doing his own stunts in Bond films he was rather coy and modest. "This is the sort of question that you should not be asking," he said. "Cinema is magic. When people pay their money and go sit inside a cinema, they must believe. And programs like this, I mean, betray all our tricks. You wouldn't expect a conjurer or a magician to give his tricks away. Now the truth of the matter is that audiences are very sophisticated now and there's been too many questions like this asked of very many films, and we know there're stuntmen and we've got a terrific team of stuntmen on this movie. Very, very highly skilled professionals led by Paul Weston. Stuntmen do stunts, and I do as much action as I can. But you must believe it's me. If you believe it's me, it's me. Otherwise and audience would feel betrayed."

(175) The 1985 film A View To A Kill was originally going to be called From a View to a Kill.

(176) Shirley Eaton, who played the doomed Jill Masterson in Goldfinger, said it was a pain trying to wash all that gold paint off her skin. "It didn't take long to get it on. About an hour I think. But getting it off was awful. I had to scrub it off with soap and water, then have several Turkish baths."

(177) George Lazenby, unless you count a Big Fry chocolate

commercial, wasn't even an actor when he became James Bond. He had rather blagged his way to an audition by pretending to be a playboy and actor. "I had no acting experience," said Lazenby. "I was coming from the male model point of view. I walked in looking like James Bond, and acting as if that's the way I was anyway. And they thought, 'All we have to do is keep this guy just the way he is and we'll have James Bond.'"

(178) The boat chase PTS in The World Is Not Enough took seven weeks to finish. Thirty-five boats were used on the production of this sequence.

(179) Pierce Brosnan first signed to play James Bond in 1986 for The Living Daylights but (much to his annoyance) had to pull out when NBC decided to reactivate Remington Steele (a cancelled TV show that Brosnan was still contracted to). "James Bond will not be Remington Steele, and Remington Steele will not be James Bond," declared Cubby Broccoli. Brosnan was replaced by Timothy Dalton in Daylights but would get his chance to play Bond again in the future.

(180) In the weapons bazaar sequence that begins Tomorrow Never Dies, the original plan was for Bond to make his way to the bazaar by ascending a frozen waterfall.

(181) It was Daniel Craig's idea for his Bond to wear Tom Ford suits.

(182) The story in Licence To Kill was inspired by Akira Kurosawa's Yojimbo (which in turn inspired films like A Fistful of Dollars). The idea was that Bond would play the villains off against one another to extract revenge for an attack on Felix Leiter.

(183) After they finished Diamonds Are Forever, the producers had the idea of bringing back Ursula Andress as Honey Ryder in the next movie. However, when Sean Connery made it clear he would not be coming back this idea was shelved. There

wasn't much point in bringing back Ursula Andress if Connery wasn't doing the movie because it wouldn't be a reunion anymore.

(184) When he auditioned to play James Bond, George Lazenby accidentally broke the nose of stuntman/wrestler Yuri Borienko with a wild punch during the fight scene part his audition. George Lazenby seemed like someone who could handle himself in a real fight and this obviously impressed the Bond people.

(185) The scene in Goldeneye where Bond uses the ejector seat to escape from the helicopter before it is struck by missiles is very similar to a scene in Die Hard 2.

(186) The lowest kill count Bond has in any movie is The Man with the Golden Gun. Bond only kills one person in the film.

(187) The Australian actor Alex O'Loughlin auditioned to play Bond in Casino Royale. O'Loughlin would go on to star in the television reboot of Hawaii Five-0.

(188) George Lazenby famously quit the Bond franchise after making only one film. The most remarkable thing about Lazenby's departure from Bond is that he genuinely seemed to believe he was leaving a sinking ship. His agent Ronan O'Rahilly told him that James Bond was conservative and out of vogue. A dust shrouded relic of the fifties that would wheeze on for a couple more films and then be consigned to cinematic history. It was one of the stupidest pieces of advice anyone could ever be unfortunate enough to receive.

(189) During the production of Live and Let Die, the Bond team had to pay 'protection' money to shoot in a rough part of Harlem.

(190) Terence Young said the jet pack in Thunderball was a very dangerous contraption because when it ran out of fuel it would simply plummet and there was no parachute.

(191) Amazingly, speculation about Timothy Dalton's future as James Bond began before the dust had even settled on Licence To Kill. The British tabloids ran stories in the summer of 1989 that the studio wanted to replace Dalton with Pierce Brosnan. The shadow of Brosnan increasingly loomed over Timothy Dalton's Bond so heavily that in 1990 a number of people noted that a (soon to be discontinued) cover on John Gardner's latest Bond novel Brokenclaw seemed to illustrate James Bond to look like Pierce Brosnan!

(192) Stars of The Avengers TV show (in its various incarnations) who appeared in Bond films are Diana Rigg, Honour Blackman, Joanna Lumley, and Patrick Macnee.

(193) George Lazenby was chosen because of his physical similarities to Connery and given the tropes of the cinematic Bond (tuxedo, casinos, Dom Pérignon etc) but Roger Moore was a different kettle of fish. It was the franchise that had to change to accommodate Moore - not the other way around.

(194) Rick van Nutter, who played Felix Leiter in Thunderball, was signed up for three films but they never actually used him again in the end.

(195) Stanley Baker's widow claimed that her late husband was offered the part of James Bond before Sean Connery but turned it down because he didn't want to be tied to a long contract. Stanley Baker is best known for the classic historical war movie Zulu.

(196) The director Terence Young said that Sean Connery could easily have been killed shooting the scene in Dr No where Bond drives between the crane. "He's very lucky to be alive. We damn near killed him. When we rehearsed it, he drove about five or ten miles an hour, just to see if he could go under it, and he cleared it by about four inches. But as we were shooting it, he was coming at forty, fifty miles an hour —and he suddenly realized the car was bouncing two feet up in the

air, and there he was with his head sticking out. It so happened that the last bounce came just before he reached the thing and he went down and under — or he would've been killed."

(197) The interesting thing about On Her Majesty's Secret Service is that it showed the Bond formula was more flexible than might have been suspected. Compared to gargantuan tongue-in-cheek extravaganzas like Thunderball and You Only Live Twice, OHMSS was surprisingly dramatic and emotional. It presented Bond not as an indestructible superhero but as someone who could have his heart broken. OHMSS was the first film in the franchise that explored the concept of making Bond more human.

(198) The Living Daylights was called Death Is Not A Game in France.

(199) Former professional rally driver Mark Higgins drove the DB5 as Bond in the Italy chase sequence in No Time To Die. He'd worked on previous films like Skyfall and Spectre. The car was specially built for the chase sequence with modern suspension and a new engine. As much as possible was done for real (as opposed to CGI). Some shots had to be done fifteen times to get them right. The chase was done on constrictive cobbled streets and required expert driving. All the cars used in the chase had BMW M3 engines. A total of seven DB5s were required to complete this sequence. One of the cars was driven via remote control so that Daniel Craig could merely simulate driving the car without having to worry about ACTUALLY having to steer and drive the car.

(200) Dr No made nearly $60 million from a budget of only one million.

(201) The Aston Martin for No Time To Die was modified by special effects coordinator and Bond veteran Chris Corbould. A number of new gadgets for the car were floated (like drones) but many of these were rejected. Bond's Aston Martin DB5

now has GE M134 Minigun-style weapons mounted behind the headlights.

(202) The design company MK12 did the title sequence for Quantum of Solace rather than regular titles designer Daniel Kleinman. Their effort seemed to lack something and it was a relief to most Bond fans when Kleinman came back for Skyfall.

(203) Only two children have ever had a speaking role in a Bond film. This happened in Diamonds Are Forever and The Man with the Golden Gun.

(204) When George Lazenby replaced Sean Connery as Bond, they were going to say that Bond had had plastic surgery to fool his enemies as a means to explain why James Bond didn't look like Sean Connery anymore. However, this idea was sensibly abandoned in the end. Audiences were well aware that the actor had changed.

(205) The Living Daylights received a fairly positive reception from critics with most of them feeling that Timothy Dalton was a welcome change of gear after thirteen years of Roger Moore. Dalton was praised by many critics for bringing the series back to earth and providing a more straight-laced interpretation of the character. Not everyone was won over though. Robert Ebert in particular seemed to think that Dalton was far too serious and lacked the charisma of Connery and the wit of Moore. A few other critics also complained that Dalton wasn't as good as Sean Connery - which felt like a rather unfair comparison. No one could ever be as good as Sean Connery was as Bond!

(206) US Magazine asked its readers in 1983 to vote for who they thought the next Bond should be. The poll was won by Pierce Brosnan in a landslide with 46% of the vote. In second place with 11% was Lewis Collins. Other names who earned votes from readers were Tom Selleck, Ian Oglivy, and Mel Gibson.

(207) Hacked Sony emails revealed that the budget for Spectre threatened to balloon to $300 million at one point.

(208) One of the sources of friction between Cubby Broccoli and Harry Saltzman was that Harry produced other projects outside Bond (like the Harry Palmer series with Michael Caine for instance) while Cubby was happy to simply focus on Bond.

(209) Gerry Anderson (of Thunderbirds fame) was asked by Harry Saltzman to develop a movie based on Fleming's Moonraker in the early 1970s but this project obviously didn't happen in the end. In 2009, Anderson said - "What happened was that Harry Saltzman phoned me and said 'Can you pop in? I'd like to see you'. I went in and he said 'Gerry, I want you to produce the next Bond picture, Moonraker – here's the book'. I nearly took off and went into orbit! I just thought it was a marvellous, marvellous break. I read the book, which frankly wasn't very exciting, and terribly out-of-date, as one would expect. I was initially trying to cement the deal, and at that time I would have put my thoughts together. What happened was that Tony Barwick – the late Tony Barwick, one of my favourite writers – and myself had written a synopsis. Harry had seen the synopsis and that was the reason he called me – he was fired by it. But a few weeks went by and then just the worst bit of luck in my life, I think! It was announced that Harry Saltzman was parting company with Cubby Broccoli. And so the thing went down the tubes."

(210) Roger Moore said that when he made Live and Let Die it was obvious to him that the relationship between Cubby Broccoli and Harry Saltzman was strained and probably not destined to last for much longer.

(211) Sean Connery said he only ever read two James Bond novels. He liked Ian Fleming as a person but didn't care for the Bond books much.

(212) Benicio del Toro cut Timothy Dalton's hand quite badly shooting a scene where Bond is captured in Licence To Kill.

(213) Rosa Kleb has a knife blade in her shoe in From Russia with Love. Believe it or not, this was a real weapon (or gadget if you prefer) used by the KGB.

(214) The 2006 film Casino Royale grossed $599 million from a $150 million budget.

(215) The famous crocodile stunt in Live and Let Die was a late replacement for a planned sequence where Bond nearly meets his end in a coffee bean milling machine. This would appear to explain why they go to great lengths early on in the film to show that Bond has an espresso coffee machine in his flat. It was meant to anticipate the punchline of a later sequence.

(216) At one point during the shooting of For Your Eyes Only, they actually slipped an outtake of Carole Bouquet into a scene because they were finding it so difficult to get her to smile! The outtake moment was of Bouquet laughing at a cheeky joke by Roger Moore.

(217) The PTS for Spectre takes place at the Day of the Dead festival. This is a real Mexican national holiday.

(218) Six different cars were used for the spectacular Lotus chase/underwater sequence in The Spy Who Loved Me. A three foot model of the car was also used.

(219) You could argue that On Her Majesty's Secret Service is the best James Bond film ever made. In 2013, the film director Steven Soderbergh went into bat for OHMSS and argued this very case when he said - "Shot to shot, this movie is beautiful in a way none of the other Bond films are — the anamorphic compositions are relentlessly arresting — and the editing patterns of the action sequences are totally bananas; it's like Peter Hunt took all the ideas of the French new wave and blended them with Eisenstein in a Cuisinart to create a grammar that still tops today's how fast can you cut aesthetic, because the difference here is that each of the shots — no

matter how short — are real shots, not just additional coverage from the hosing-it-down school of action, so there is a unification of the aesthetic of the first unit and the second unit that doesn't exist in any other Bond film. And, speaking of action, there are as many big set pieces in OHMSS as any Bond film ever made, and if that weren't enough, there's a great score by John Barry, some really striking sound work, and what can you say about Diana Rigg that doesn't start with the word WOW?"

(220) Pierce Brosnan found himself in the wars shooting Tomorrow Never dies. He had to endure a bout of influenza and then needed stitches when a protective helmet worn by a stuntman hit him in the face.

(221) Roger Moore said he had a Tarot card reading when he made Live and Let Die. The cards predicted he would perish in an accident involving a black car. Roger said he avoided black cars for quite a long time after that reading!

(222) Blofeld's mountain base Piz Gloria in On Her Majesty's Secret Service was an under construction restaurant high on a mountain near Interlaken. You could only get there by cable car. The Bond producers were given permission to use the building in return for constructing new interiors. Hundreds of tons of concrete had to be taken to the site to build a helicopter landing pad.

(223) The British government only acknowledged the existence of MI6 in 1986.

(224) Pierce Brosnan was the first Bond to wear an Omega watch.

(225) Jill St John and Lana Wood play Bond girls in Diamonds Are Forever. There was a strange connection between these women some years later. Jill St John later married Robert Wagner. Wagner used to be married to Lana's sister Natalie Wood. Natalie Wood drowned in 1981 while on a yacht with

Robert Wagner and Lana has always suspected foul play in her sister's death. There is another bizarre Bond connection to this story because the third person on the yacht that tragic night was Christopher Walken.

(226) During production on Dr No, Sean Connery took a dozen takes to throw Bond's hat on the coat tree in Moneypenny's office. He got much better at this as the films went on.

(227) Making a Bond film represents a fairly unique physical and mental challenge for an actor. Production lasts about six months and as James Bond is obviously going to be in virtually every scene you can't expect to get many days off. Factor in the stunts, fight scenes, and generally getting battered and smashed around and you can see why Daniel Craig in particular came to enjoy making a new Bond film about as much as a trip to the dentist.

(228) Roger Moore said he loved making Moonraker in France because the French crew didn't start work until noon!

(229) Bond driving a humble Citroën 2CV for a chase in For Your Eyes Only is a very pointed reaction to the fact that critics had complained about the Bond films becoming too gadget festooned and outlandish.

(230) Lani Hall said she didn't like her Never Say Never Again title song very much.

(231) If anywhere can be called the physical home of James Bond it is Pinewood Studios. Pinewood is a film and television studio located in the village of Iver Heath in Buckinghamshire.

(232) Sammy Davis Jr. shot a cameo for Diamonds are Forever but the director Guy Hamilton decided to axe it from the movie.

(233) Noel Coward, who was a neighbour of Ian Fleming, was offered the part of Dr No.

(234) Patrick McGoohan, star of Danger Man and The Prisoner, was approached to play Bond in Dr No but ruled himself out on moral grounds. "It has an insidious and powerful influence on children," he said. "Would you like your son to grow up like James Bond? Since I hold these views strongly as an individual and parent I didn't see how I could contribute to the very things to which I objected."

(235) Robert Shaw dyed his hair to play Red Grant in from Russia with Love. He also hit the gym because he wanted Red Grant to seem like Bond's physical equal.

(236) One of the most surprising additions to the cast in Licence To Kill is the crooner Wayne Newton as the TV evangelist Joe Butcher. Newton had apparently contacted Cubby Broccoli and said he'd always wanted to be in a Bond film. Broccoli granted his wish. Newton based Joe Butcher on Jimmy Swaggart. Jimmy Swaggart is an American Pentecostal evangelist who has been on TV and radio for years. Newton ad-libbed much of Joe Butcher's dialogue in Licence To Kill.

(237) The end of Diamonds Are Forever was supposed to feature a confrontation between Bond and Blofeld in a salt mine. However, they couldn't get permission to shoot in any local mines so they abandoned this idea.

(238) In his novel You Only Live Twice, Fleming says that James Bond weighs 183 pounds.

(239) Caroline Munro was cast as Naomi in The Spy who Loved Me after Cubby Broccoli saw her picture as part of the Lambs Navy Rum campaign. Munro was also known for her association with Hammer Horror films.

(240) The plot of the movie Quantum of Solace was partly inspired by the Cochabamba Water War. The Cochabamba Water War was a series of protests that took place in Cochabamba, Bolivia's fourth largest city, between December

1999 and April 2000 in response to the privatization of the city's municipal water supply company SEMAPA.

(241) It took twenty-nine takes to shoot the moment in Live and Let Die when Bond unzips Miss Caruso's dress with his magnetic watch.

(242) When The Living Daylights was released, The Washington Post's Desson Howe wrote of Timothy Dalton - 'He's spindly but energetic and enthusiastic. The eyes are scintillating, green and squinty. The accent's as refined as Moore's, but free of aloofness. He doesn't have the hairy-chested exuberance of Connery, but there's a warmth trying to get out.'

(243) Fleming's literary James Bond dislikes killing (despite it obviously being an unavoidable part of his job). 'It was part of his profession to kill people. He had never liked doing it and when he had to kill he did it as well as he knew how and forgot about it. As a secret agent who held the rare double-O prefix - the licence to kill in the Secret Service - it was his duty to be as cool about death as a surgeon. If it happened, it happened. Regret was unprofessional - worse, it was death-watch beetle in the soul.'

(244) The headaches of the costume department on a Bond film were illustrated by the fact there were 33 versions of one of Bond's Tom Ford suits for No Time To Die. The different versions were needed for Daniel Craig, his stunt double, stunt drivers, visual effects, and then to depict various stages of wear and tear.

(245) The end of Live and Let Die, with the (seemingly ghostly) Baron Samedi on the front of the train, was included with a view to bringing the character back but this obviously never happened in the end.

(246) The character of Christmas Jones in The World Is Not Enough was going to be a bounty hunter at one point but then

became a nuclear scientist.

(247) Ilse Steppat, who played Irma Bunt in On Her Majesty's Secret Service, died only four days after the film was released.

(248) Terence Young was supposed to direct Goldfinger but he left during pre-production after a dispute over his salary. He was replaced by Guy Hamilton. Hamilton had turned down the first Bond film Dr No.

(249) When the first James Bond film was being planned, Ian Fleming sent Broccoli and Saltzman a memo with his own thoughts about the approach they should take. 'Atmosphere: To my mind, the greatest danger in this series is too much stage Englishness,' wrote Fleming. 'There should, I think, be no monocles, mustaches, bowler hats or bobbies or other "Limey" gimmicks. There should be no blatant English slang, a minimum of public school ties and accents.'

(250) The early version of You Only Live Twice was three hours long and received negative feedback from just about everyone who viewed it. It was the editor Peter Hunt who savaged the film and managed to cut it down to a more manageable length without affecting the coherence too much (not that this is probably the most coherent Bond film anyway).

(251) Maurice Binder's title sequence for Licence To Kill uses Former Playboy Playmate Diane Hsu to good effect. Hsu also has a small role in the film as Hong Kong Narcotics Agent Loti.

(252) In a publicity stunt, Sean Connery arrived at the first French screening of Goldfinger in an Aston Martin. He was very irritated when a woman raced from the crowd and jumped in the car with him.

(253) The end of Diamonds Are Forever was originally going to be longer and have Bond in pursuit of Blofeld (after Blofeld has fled the oil rig) by hanging onto the rope from a hot air

balloon.

(254) The brilliant train fight in From Russia with Love between Bond and Robert Shaw's Red Grant took three weeks to shoot.

(255) One of the extras at Felix Leiter's wedding in Licence To Kill was a woman named Sandi Sentell. Sentell had won a competition to appear in a Bond film.

(256) Near the start of Diamonds are Forever, M tells Bond that, contrary to what he might have presumed, the secret service does function in his absence. This is an in-joke referencing that fact that Connery is back after a one film hiatus.

(257) Theodore Bikel was strongly considered for the part of Auric Goldfinger. You can actually watch his screen test on YouTube.

(258) The PTS freefall in Moonraker required over 90 jumps before sufficient footage was in the can. The parachutists could only film very limited footage on each jump.

(259) The original plan for the cargo plane sequence in The Living Daylights was for Bond to land the cargo plane on an aircraft carrier.

(260) The helicopter PTS in For Your Eyes Only was shot at the abandoned Beckton Gas Works in London. This was where Stanley Kubrick later shot parts of Full Metal Jacket.

(261) In 1971, as Diamonds Are Forever geared up for release, Sean Connery said of Cubby Broccoli and Harry Saltzman - "They're not exactly enamoured of each other. Probably because they're both sitting on fifty million dollars or pounds and looking across the desk at each other and thinking: that bugger's got half of what should be all mine."

(262) James Mason was supposed to play Hugo Drax in Moonraker but because the production was moved to Paris (due high tax rates in Britain at the time) a quota of French actors had to be cast and so Michael Lonsdale got the part of Drax instead.

(263) The Living Daylights grossed about $190 million worldwide. It was up against the teen vampire horror comedy The Lost Boys at the US box-office but had an $11 million weekend to claim the top spot.

(264) The motorbike chase in Never Say Never Again was supposed to be much more spectacular. The bike was supposed to have 'wings' which came out to make it capable of leaping over trucks and small buildings. Much to the annoyance of director Irvin Kershner though, this bike chase was made much more modest in the end thanks to budget cuts.

(265) The composer Bill Conti tried to get Barbara Streisand or Donna Summer to sing the theme son to For Your Eyes Only. Sheena Easton got the gig in the end.

(266) The Cuban-born Venezuelan-American actress Maria Conchita Alonso (who unsuccessfully auditioned for the part of Fatima Blush in Never Say Never Again) was the original choice for the part of Lupe Lamora in Licence To Kill. However, after accepting the part, Alonso then had a change of heart and dropped out of the film.

(267) A deleted scene in Dr No had Honey Ryder tied up as bait for giant crabs. They axed this sequence because they thought it lacked tension and drama.

(268) The Living Daylights was called The Iron Curtain in Romania.

(269) The little boy who points at Bond's Lotus as it drives out of the sea in The Spy Who Loved Me is Richard (Jaws) Kiel's

son.

(270) You Only Live Twice was called One Doesn't Live More Than Twice in France.

(271) Timothy Dalton's era marked the last contributions of the great composer John Barry, screenwriter Richard Maibaum, titles designer Maurice Binder, actor Robert Brown as M, and in-house director John Glen to the series. The Living Daylights was also notably the last true Cold War James Bond film produced.

(272) Peter Hunt said he was asked to come back and direct another Bond after On Her Majesty's Secret Service but the timing was always unlucky. They always seemed to ask him when he was busy on another film.

(273) To save money, Licence To Kill was based at a Mexican Studio rather than Pinewood because tax rates in Britain at the time were not favourable. However, the production in Mexico had so many logistical problems that it would have been cheaper in the end to shoot all the interior scenes at Pinewood!

(274) Peter Hunt, director and editor on the early Bond films, feels that Dr No was a success because it was so different from the other films being made in Britain at the time. "You must remember that the climate of the audiences at the time was very kitchen sink. It was all for actresses doing the washing up, and the housework, the sleazy back room about hard lives, which I guess the audience had become a bit bored with. Here was an absolute breath of fantasy, glamour, and they loved it."

(275) One of the best reviews for The Living Daylights and Timothy Dalton came from Rita Kempley in The Washington Post. 'The best Bond ever,' she wrote. 'He's as classy as the trademark tuxedo, as sleek as the Aston Martin. Like Bond's notorious martini, women who encounter his carved-granite good looks are shaken, not stirred.'

(276) Jaclyn Smith was the first choice for the role of Holly Goodhead in Moonraker but she couldn't do it in the end because of a production clash with her television show Charlie's Angels.

(277) Roger Moore had to go to a bus depot in London to learn how to drive a double-decker bus before he made Live and Let Die.

(278) The Bond franchise has had to compete with an eclectic and constant number of action films and franchises over the decades. Many of these films and franchises were inspired by Bond themselves. The list of films and franchises the Bond series, over many decades, has had to keep pace with is endless and varied. Dirty Harry, Enter the Dragon, Rambo, Lethal Weapon, Superman, Die Hard, Mad Max, Arnold Schwarzenegger movies, John Woo, Speed, Mission Imossible, Batman, The Matrix, Derek Flint, Matt Helm, Bulldog Drummond, Remo Williams, The Long Kiss Goodnight, Lara Croft, xXx, Jack Ryan, Jackie Chan, Stormbreaker, The Peacemaker, Fast and the Furious, Marvel, John Wick, Taken. No other franchise or action character though has been as enduring as James Bond.

(279) Guy Green turned down a chance to direct Dr No. Green was a cinematographer turned director.

(280) Nikki Van der Zyl did a lot of dubbing on the Bond films from the early days through to Moonraker. She even did some ADR for Jane Seymour in Live and Let Die. Automated dialogue replacement is the process of re-recording dialogue by the original actor after the filming process to improve audio quality or reflect dialogue changes. Nikki Van der Zyl was an excellent mimic and impressionist. Despite her (largely unheralded) importance to the Bond franchise, she didn't get paid very well and usually got £50 a session.

(281) Goldeneye was the first Bond film not to use Pinewood because the studio had no available space at the time.

Ironically, one of the films taking up space at Pinewood was First Knight with Sean Connery.

(282) Jan Werich was originally cast by Harry Saltzman to play Blofeld in You Only Live Twice. However, when production began, the director Lewis Gilbert and Cubby Broccoli felt that Werich lacked menace so he was eventually axed and replaced with Donald Pleasance.

(283) Maryam d'Abo dubbed herself as Kara in the French language version of The Living Daylights. She was a fluent French speaker after spending her youth in Paris.

(284) The satellite dish climax in Goldeneye was filmed at the Arecibo Observatory in Puerto Rico.

(285) Die Another Day achieved the impossible by uniting Korea. North Korea complained about the North Korean villains while in South Korea there were protests against the movie for its depiction of South Korea as something akin to a colony of the United States.

(286) The main reason why Kevin McClory didn't go full steam ahead and try and make his own version of Thunderball in the 1960s is that he knew it would be impossible to find any alternative actor of the stature of Sean Connery. This was why he tried to woo Richard Burton. McClory figured that Burton was just about the next best thing but even Richard Burton probably couldn't have been as good as Connery. `

(287) There was a lot of speculation in the media that (what became) Tomorrow Never Dies was going to be called Aquator but this obviously never happened in the end.

(288) Grace Jones was allowed to design her own clothes as May Day in A View To A kill.

(289) Quantum of Solace suffered from a writer's strike. Things got so bad that even Daniel Craig did some work on the

script.

(290) John Barry makes a cameo in The Living Daylights as an orchestra conductor.

(291) Ian Fleming's literary James Bond dislikes tea. He much prefers coffee.

(292) Roger Spottiswoode was asked to direct the next Bond film after Tomorrow Never Dies but declined the offer. He said he was too tired.

(293) Austin Willis was cast as Felix Leiter in Goldfinger but swapped roles with Cec Linder - who was originally cast as a man playing cards.

(294) Mathilda May (forever immortal as the nude space vampire from Tobe Hooper's Lifeforce) unsuccessfully auditioned for the part of love interest Kara Milovy in The Living Daylights.

(295) Anthony Newley sang an alternative version of Goldfinger but they went with Shirley Bassey in the end.

(296) Len Deighton wrote the first draft of From Russia with Love. Deighton later worked on Kevin McClory's aborted Warhead film in the 1970s.

(297) Terence Young said that George Baker was a candidate to play James Bond in Dr No. Baker later played Sir Hilary Bray in On Her Majesty's Secret Service.

(298) Ken Hughes turned down the chance to direct Dr No. Hughes later directed Ian Fleming's Chitty Chitty Bang Bang for Cubby Broccoli. He was also one of many directors on the 1967 Casino Royale spoof.

(299) Ingrid Bergman's daughter Pia Lindstrom tested for the part of Tatiana in From Russia with Love.

(300) Michael Apted said that the producers asked him to direct Die Another Day but MGM meddling nixed this. "The new management un-invited me and I had this very difficult meeting with the Broccolis [Michael G. Wilson and Barbara Broccoli] where they said they had to un-invite me. [Metro-Goldwyn-Mayer] thought, "We can do better than him. We want to put our mark on it. We can get Tony Scott or John Woo and they couldn't." They came back to me, but by that time I had got another job. So that was unfortunate because I would have loved to have done another one."

(301) GoldenEye grossed $355 million from a $60 million budget.

(302) Michael France's early draft of the Goldeneye script had an interesting concept at its heart which managed to survive various revisions by later writers and remain in the actual film. France's big idea was to have another Double O agent in the story. "It occurred to me," said France, "that we`d never really seen Bond interacting with another Double O sector agent. In the rest of the series, they are nameless, faceless characters. M says, '003 got killed in Malaysia but he sent us this expository note', or something, and the story would move on with just a slight reaction from Bond, if any at all. That seemed false to me. I thought Bond would have very good friends in the sector - that they`d be as tight as men who go into combat together -- and I thought it would really be something to build up that kind of relationship and make a Double O agent the villain."

(303) Legend has it that Harry Saltzman didn't like Shirley Bassey's Goldfinger song. Harry was apparently quite famous for having a tin ear when it came to music.

(304) John Barry didn't care much for his score for The Man with the Golden Gun. "It's the one I hate most ... it just never happened for me."

(305) If one excludes George Lazenby (who only made one

film and had a purely instrumental theme), Pierce Brosnan is the only Bond actor who never had a male vocalist sing the theme song to any of his films.

(306) There were plans for a big bazaar sequence in The Living Daylights but this didn't get shot in the end. This idea seems to have been later recycled and used in the PTS of Tomorrow Never Dies a decade later.

(307) The steel teeth Richard Kiel wore to play Jaws were very uncomfortable. They made him want to retch if left in for too long.

(308) The first screen adaptation of James Bond was a 1954 CBS version of Casino Royale as part of Climax Mystery Theater. Barry Nelson portrayed 'Jimmy' Bond - an American card shark. This one hour production obviously wasn't tremendously faithful to Ian Fleming.

(309) Fleming's short story Quantum of Solace has nothing in common with the 2008 film. The short story has Bond dining with the Governor of the Bahamas and listening to a yarn about an airline attendant.

(310) Thunderball was called Calm Down, Mr Bond in Holland.

(311) 1984, the year before Roger Moore's last Bond film was released, saw a number of rumours that Pierce Brosnan was going to be the new Bond. An Australian newspaper published an article in which they said Brosnan had already signed a secret deal to replace Roger. Brosnan had to deny these rumours and even wrote to Cubby Broccoli assuring him that these stories did not originate from him or anyone connected to him.

(312) Timothy Dalton made the decision not to return as James Bond in 1994. Litigation had mothballed the series from 1989 but now plans were gearing up for a new movie

(that would of course become Goldeneye). Many years later Dalton said that his decision was prompted by the fact that he only wanted to come back and make one more film whereas EON didn't see the point of this. "Cubby Broccoli asked if I would come back," said Dalton, "and I said, 'Well, I've actually changed my mind a little bit. I think that I'd love to do one. Try and take the best of the two that I have done, and consolidate them into a third.' And he said, quite rightly, 'Look, Tim. You can't do one. There's no way, after a five-year gap between movies that you can come back and just do one. You'd have to plan on four or five.' And I thought, oh, no, that would be the rest of my life. Too much. Too long. So I respectfully declined."

(313) Geoffrey Holder, who played Baron Samedi, also choreographed the voodoo scenes in Live and Let Die.

(314) Kevin McClory harboured ambitions to direct the 1965 EON version of Thunderball but this rather unlikely to happen.

(315) Skyfall is the first Bond film to feature Q and Moneypenny since Die Another Day 10 years previously.

(316) Denis Richards won a Golden Raspberry for her performance as Christmas Jones in The World Is Not Enough.

(317) Lois Maxwell's daughter Melinda Maxwell played one of Drax's girls in Moonraker.

(318) The South American heroin plant in the Goldfinger PTS was shot at a disused gasworks in London.

(319) For Your Eyes Only was called Agent 007: Strict Confidence in Denmark.

(320) Sean Connery apparently picked up his love of golf playing the game with Gert Frobe while they made Goldfinger.

(321) Roger Moore didn't like the scene in The Man with the

Golden Gun where Bond roughs up Maud Adams.

(322) 400 actresses were considered for the part of Camille Montes in Quantum of Solace.

(323) In his novel From Russia with Love, Fleming says that Tatiana Romanova based her hairstyle on Greta Garbo.

(324) Guy Hamilton said he didn't like Yaphet Kotto very much when he directed Live and Let Die. "Yaphet Kotto, I regret bitterly. I did not enjoy working with him at all. Originally it was to be a very distinguished American black actor. Suddenly Harry Saltzman announced he's out and UA say Yaphet Kotto is really hot property. We were forced into Yaphet Kotto. I'd never met him until he turned up on the set. He starts off thinking he should be playing Bond - quite seriously. He was very badly behaved, he would try and make life difficult."

(325) A graphic novel adaptation of Licence To Kill was released by Eclipse Books. This adaptation is rather confusing to follow if you aren't very familiar with the film. The main problem with the graphic novel is that Timothy Dalton refused permission for his likeness to be used and the illustrations of James Bond are never consistent in the book. The visual depiction of James Bond in the graphic novel frequently changes - to the point you are occasionally confused as to who he is supposed to be!

(326) The early version of Goldeneye by Michael France was literally wall to wall action at times. In fact, so festooned with action was France's draft that EON later took out several action scenes and 'banked' them to use in later films (much to the public irritation of France). The most obvious example is the scene in The World Is Not Enough where the helicopters attack with buzzsaws chained underneath. This sequence was in Michael France's Goldeneye draft. The buzzsaw scenes are so similar that they had to give France a writing credit on The World Is Not Enough.

(327) The one James Bond film that cried out for a direct continuation, On Her Majesty's Secret Service, did not get one. OHMSS ends with the death of Bond's wife. However, in the next film, Diamonds Are Forever, Sean Connery was back in place of George Lazenby and Bond's 'revenge' on Blofeld for the death of his wife is confined to the pre-title sequence. It is not even established though whether Connery's Bond is the same Bond who went through the events of OHMSS.

(328) The Living Daylights was called Spies Die At Dawn in Denmark.

(329) When Pierce Brosnan was released after Die Another Day, Judi Dench was the only cast regular from the Brosnan films to feature in the Daniel Craig era. John Cleese, Colin Salmon, Samantha Bond, and Michael Kitchen were not used again. The producers obviously decided that it would be hard to do any better than Dame Judi Dench so kept her in place. It seems unlikely that the M played by Dench in the Brosnan films can be the same M played Dench in the Craig films.

(330) In a 2017 interview for the Money into Light blog, Ted Kotcheff (of First Blood fame) said he was offered Bond 17 (when Timothy Dalton was still set to play Bond) but turned it down because the proposed fee was too low. "It was the only time that I turned down a movie over money. I thought 'If I'm going to do a Bond movie, I want to get paid.' Nobody is going to look at a Bond film and say 'Oh, what a great directorial job.' On a Bond film what you need is a good stunt co-ordinator. It's too bad. I do like the series, and I love Sean Connery in particular."

(331) John Rhys-Davies was offered a chance to return as General Pushkin in Licence To Kill but he declined the offer because he was too busy shooting Indiana Jones and the Last Crusade.

(332) The director Guy Hamilton said he didn't like The Man

with the Golden Gun very much. After making three Bond films in a row, Hamilton said he felt exhausted and bereft of ideas on Golden Gun.

(333) Robert Davi improvised the Sanchez line "Loyalty is more important to me than money" in Licence To Kill.

(334) Believe it or not, George Lazenby came on the radar of EON when Cubby Broccoli noticed him in his hairdressers.

(335) Pierce Brosnan said he didn't enjoy making Tomorrow Never dies very much because there were so many script problems and it was a rather rushed production thanks to a tight release date. Both Jonathan Pryce and Judi Dench complained when the script they'd read and learned was completely changed at the last minute - requiring them to learn their lines all over again.

(336) A View To A Kill was called The Prospect of Death in Czech.

(337) When a Bond film came out, Cubby Broccoli liked to go to cinemas and watch the film with an audience so he could guage what worked and what didn't. He was always very interested to see which jokes worked and which didn't.

(338) Regarding the introduction of Bond's Aston Martin into the movie franchise, production designer Ken Adam said - "I had an E-type Jaguar in the 60s and I remember the debate about which sports car Bond should drive. We decided on the sexiest British sports car at the time and John Stears from special effects and myself went to Newport Pagnall, where they made Aston Martins, and they weren't at all helpful. Reluctantly, after the big boys from the studio stepped in, they let us have two, but after the Bond film their sales went up by 47% and there were no problems getting cars after that. I never owned one myself - if I remember correctly the clutch wasn't all that good."

(339) The reclusive Howard Hughes allowed the producers of Diamonds Are Forever to shoot scenes in his Las Vegas casinos and hotels. In return for this, Hughes simply asked for one print of the finished film so he could watch it privately.

(340) James Bond is estimated have drunk 277 units of alcohol in the Bond movies.

(341) In the novel On Her Majesty's Secret Service, Fleming says that Bond reads The Daily Express. The Express were famous for printing a James Bond comic strip.

(342) The Australian actor Rod Taylor (best known for The Time Machine) was approached about becoming the first ever screen James Bond in 1962 but he rebuffed the interest. This was something he soon came to regret. "I refused because I thought it was beneath me," said Taylor. "I didn't think Bond would be successful in the movies. That was one of the greatest mistakes of my career! Every time a new Bond picture became a smash hit, I tore out my hair!"

(343) Roger Moore was the first Bond actor to wear a tuxedo in his gunbarrel intro.

(344) The Eiffel Tower leap in A View To A Kill was originally planned for Moonraker.

(345) Solitaire's real name in the Bond books is Simone Latrelle.

(346) According to writers Dick Clement and Ian La Frenais, the script and production of Never Say Never Again was so amateurish that the crew started shooting scenes in the Bahamas without the script having any explanation whatsoever for why Bond should be in the Bahamas! They had to add an explanation into the script.

(347) Roger Moore, very shrewdly as it turned out, rejected Lew Grade's offer to sign up for a second season on The

Persuaders because he had a feeling the Bond role would be vacant again soon.

(348) It was very difficult to shoot the gondola sequence in Moonraker because Venice was full of tourists and they kept rushing up to take photographs of Roger Moore and the Bond production.

(349) The title sequence for On Her Majesty's Secret Service connects to the past by showing us clips of characters from the Connery films. The intention is to assure us that while the Bond actor has changed this is still the same character.

(350) Duran Duran's A View to a Kill was the first Bond theme to hit No. 1 on the Billboard Top 100.

(351) It seems evident from interviews with Martin Campbell that EON would have happily allowed him to become the modern day version of John Glen and direct as many films as he'd wanted to after GoldenEye and perhaps even Casino Royale. "I don't know if it was sort of arrogance or whatever I don't know," said Campbell, "I just sort of said no to it. I was pretty much offered every one after GoldenEye. But I just felt that I was repeating it. Another control room to blow up; another nutcase taking over the world. Also there is something refreshing about starting a new Bond, and particularly with Pierce [Brosnan]. It was sort of a Cold War sort of situation then, and we had Judi Dench for the first time. So there was a kind of excitement to doing it. Casino Royale was the same thing. Much the same reasons, actually."

(352) No Time to Die director Cary Fukunaga said it was weird to complete a film but then not know when it could be released. He must have felt like Terry Gilliam after he'd made Brazil!

(353) Pierce Brosnan said that he avoided The Living Daylights like the plague when it came out. It was simply too painful to be reminded of the film he was supposed to star in.

Brosnan couldn't avoid the film forever though and said he eventually encountered Daylights while part of a captive audience on a plane!

(354) When they were looking for someone to replace Sean Connery in On Her Majesty's Secret Service, United Artists boss David Picker suggested the Australian tennis ace John Newcombe might be a good candidate! Thankfully, nothing came of this.

(355) Carole Bouquet suffered from sinus problems and couldn't do any underwater scenes in For Your Eyes Only. They used the magic of movies to make it appear that her character Melina was underwater.

(356) Tomorrow Never Dies was supposed to be called Tomorrow Never Lies. Legend has it a studio fax was misread as Dies rather than Lies and the new title just stuck for some reason.

(357) Akiko Wakabyashi and Mie Hama swapped roles in You Live Only Live Twice when it was discovered that Hama's English was better.

(358) Ian Fleming based the plot of Casino Royale on an incident that happened to him in real life. 'I was on my way to America with the Director of Naval Intelligence, Admiral Godfrey. We were in Estoril in Portugal, and while we were waiting for transport, we killed some time in the casino. While there, I recognised some German agents, and I thought it would be a brilliant coup to play with them, break them, take their money. Instead, of course, they took mine. Most embarrassing. This incident appears in Casino Royale, my first book – but, of course, Bond does not lose. In fact, he totally and coldly vanquishes his opponent.'

(359) Irvin Kershner, the director of Never Say Never Again, said that many planned sequences either had to be scrapped or scaled down because of the lack of money. He felt as if he

always had one arm tied behind his back on that movie and that it could have been much better with a bigger budget.

(360) Live and Let Die is one of the few films where Bond and Leiter have a believable easygoing chemistry. This is because Roger Moore and David Hedison were friends in real life.

(361) Ian Fleming's James Bond began working for the British Secret Service in 1938.

(362) The Bond series was hugely influential on the many villains we've seen in action films through the decades. Alan Rickman's Hans Gruber in Die Hard is like the best Bond villain we never got. Shih Kien as the steel handed baddie Han in Enter the Dragon is patently a Bond inspired villain.

(363) Dr No, the first Bond movie, was called Licence To Kill in Italy.

(364) Bryan Forbes turned the chance to direct Dr No. Forbes directed such films as Whistle Down the Wind, Séance on a Wet Afternoon, and The Stepford Wives.

(365) Roger Moore received racist hate mail because of his kissing scenes with black actress Gloria Hendry in Live and Let Die.

(366) Gloria Hendry said that Roger Moore was an absolute gentleman on the set of Live and Let Die. He even shared his chauffeur driven limousine with her.

(367) The Hamburg car chase in Tomorrow Never Dies (where Bond deploys his remote control BMW) was shot at Brent Cross Shopping Centre in London.

(368) Dick Clement and Ian La Frenais, who were brought in as writers three weeks into the shooting of Never Say Never Again, estimate that 30% of the script was then rewritten as the film was shot. This was obviously not an ideal situation for

any film.

(369) When he was 24, Timothy Dalton was invited to a James
Bond casting call for On Her Majesty's Secret Service. Dalton
however didn't turn up to the casting call and had no interest
in playing James Bond at the time. "When Sean Connery gave
up the role," said Dalton, years later, "I guess I, alongside quite
a few other actors, was approached about the possibility of
playing the part. That was for OHMSS. I was very flattered,
but I think anybody would have been off their head to have
taken over from Connery. I was also too young. Bond should
be a man in his mid-30s, at least - a mature adult who has
been around."

(370) The popular children's author Roald Dahl wrote the
movie version of You Only Live Twice. Dahl met Ian Fleming
during the war and the pair had been friends. Not much of the
novel was retained in the film treatment.

"You Only Live Twice was the only Fleming book that had
virtually no semblance of a plot that could be made into a
movie," said Dahl. "The concept of Blofeld patrolling his
garden of poisonous plants in a medieval suit of armor [sic]
and lopping off the heads of half-blinded Japanese was
ridiculous. When I began the script, I could retain only four or
five of the original novel's story ideas. Obviously, the movie
had to take place in Japan. We kept Blofeld and Tiger Tanaka
and Bond's pearl-diving girlfriend, Kissy Suzuki. And we
retained the Ninjas – those masters of oriental martial arts
who use their talents to raid Blofeld's hideout. But aside from
those bits, I had nothing except a wonderful Ian Fleming title."

(371) Desmond Llewelyn asked for a farewell scene for Q in the
Bond movies because he wanted a dignified exit (as opposed to
EON simply keep using him until he passed away). He was
supposed to say farewell in Tomorrow Never Dies but in the
end he made his final bow in The World Is Not Enough. Sadly,
Llewelyn died not long after the film came out.

(372) That's really Timothy Dalton on top of the jeep in the PTS for The Living Daylights. They strapped Dalton to the top so he couldn't fall off.

(373) In the short story 007 in New York, Fleming shares Bond's theory on how to make perfect scrambled eggs. 'Break the eggs into a bowl. Beat thoroughly with a fork and season well. In a small copper (or heavy bottomed saucepan) melt four oz. of the butter. When melted, pour in the eggs and cook over a very low heat, whisking continuously with a small egg whisk. While the eggs are slightly more moist than you would wish for eating, remove the pan from heat, add rest of butter and continue whisking for half a minute, adding the while finely chopped chives or fines herbes. Serve on hot buttered toast in individual copper dishes (for appearance only) with pink champagne (Taittinger) and low music.'

(374) A big Aston Martin chase sequence was shot in Matera for No Time To Die. 8,400 gallons of Coca-Cola were used to make a street in Maratea less slippery for a motorbike and car stunt (the coke left a sticky residue and so gave the bike and car more grip). Barbara Broccoli thought the stunt crew had gone mad when she saw that they'd covered the road in Coca-Cola so they had to explain to her why they'd done this and why they were spending a sizeable little chunk of the budget on preposterous amounts of this popular soft-drink. £55,000 was spent on Coca-Cola for this sequence. Coca-Cola, according to the stunt director, actually washed off very easily and made the streets look cleaner than they were before.

(375) In the film Never Say Never Again, Edward Fox's references his 'illustrious predecessor'. This appears to be a reference to Bernard Lee's M in the official EON movies.

(376) John Ronane was considered for the part of Bond in Live and Let Die. Ronane was best known for films like Charlie Bubbles and King Rat.

(377) It is sometimes said the OO agents in the Gibraltar

training exercise PTS of The Living Daylights are made to look like previous Bond actors but I've never noticed much obvious similarity myself! Is the foppish blond haired 002 (who gets stuck in a tree) supposed to be Roger Moore? He doesn't look like him much.

(378) If a 1983 interview he conducted with Starlog for the release of Octopussy is anything to go by, James Bond writer Richard Maibaum wasn't the biggest fan of Roger Moore's Bond. Maibaum felt the films had become too tongue-in-cheek and complained that Roger kept changing lines in the script in favour of his own quips!

(379) Never Say Never Again was supposed to begin with a sequence at a medieval pageant where one knight is killed in a jousting display. A third knight gives chase on horseback and is revealed to be 007. This sequence was never shot because they didn't have the time nor the money.

(380) Timothy Dalton said he spoke to Cubby Broccoli about becoming James Bond in the late 1970s when Roger Moore's participation in the next picture was in doubt. Dalton said he wasn't very enthusiastic at the time because he felt the Bond films had become too tongue-in-cheek and comedic.

(381) A-Ha and John Barry did not get along very well working on the Living Daylights theme. It would be fair to say that they loathed one another. There were some creative differences over the theme and A-Ha later released their own version on one of their albums. However, Barry's version was vastly superior and thankfully that's the version we got in the movie.

(382) The producers considered bringing Jaws back in For Your Eyes Only but decided in the end that he would clash with the more down to earth (for the Roger Moore era at least) tone of the film.

(383) Peter Hunt felt that George Lazenby would have made a great Bond if he'd stuck with the franchise. "Had George

Lazenby been more sensible, and had Broccoli and Saltzman been more sensible with him, I think he would have made a very credible Bond. He was a great looking guy and he moved along very well, although he wasn't really an actor. He was a model who had not done any acting before that. I think if things had gone the other way, he would have gone on to be a very good Bond."

(384) Ian Fleming said of James Bond - 'Bond is not a hero, nor is he depicted as being very likable or admirable. He is a Secret Service Agent. He's not a bad man, but he is ruthless and self-indulgent. He enjoys the fight- he also enjoys the prizes. In fiction people used to have blood in their veins. Nowadays they have pond water. My books are just out of step. But then so are all the people who read them. I didn't intend for Bond to be likable. He's a blunt instrument in the hands of the government. He's got vices and few perceptible virtues.'

(385) Bond originally shot Professor Dent six times in Dr No but the censors thought this was too violent and sadistic and ordered cuts to be made.

(386) Jack Palance was considered to play Scaramanga in The Man with the Golden Gun but he wasn't interested enough to pursue the role.

(387) Timothy Dalton shot an alternative gunbarrel opening for The Living Daylights in which he does a little jump as he turns around to fire at the screen. You can find this unused gunbarrel on YouTube quite easily and you can see why it wasn't used.

(388) GoldenEye 007 for the Nintendo 64 sold about 8 million copies.

(389) James Brolin's 007 screentest for Octopussy is easy to find on YouTube. Brolin did his test in an American accent. The director John Glen told Brolin they could work on his British accent later if he got the part.

(390) When he became James Bond, Roger Moore was already
old friends with Moneypenny actress Lois Maxwell because
they had met at Rada (the Royal Academy of Dramatic Art - a
famous drama school in London).

(391) Lynn-Holly Johnson, who plays Bibi Dahl in for Your
Eyes Only, used to be a professional ice skater.

(392) Regarding the escapist glamour of the Bond novels,
Fleming wrote - 'What I aim at is a certain disciplined
exoticism. I have not re-read any of my books to see if this
stands up to close examination, but I think you will find that
the sun is always shining in my books—a state of affairs which
minutely lifts the spirit of the English reader—that most of the
settings of my books are in themselves interesting and
pleasurable, taking the reader to exciting places around the
world, and that, in general, a strong hedonistic streak is always
there to offset the grimmer side of Bond's adventures. This, so
to speak, "pleasures" the reader.'

(393) In Fleming's novel The Man With The Golden Gun,
Bond is brainwashed by the KGB and tries to kill M. This
sequence has never made its way into the Bond films.

(394) No Time to Die was previously the name of a Columbo
episode. It was also the alternative British title of a 1958 Cubby
Broccoli produced war film called Tank Force! which starred
Victor Mature.

(395) There seems to be evidence that Cubby Broccoli and
Harry saltzman were not entirely convinced by Roger moore
and would have preferred Michael Billington to be cast as
Bond in Live and Let Die. The story goes that United Artists
did not want another unknown actor and so voted for Moore
over Billington. The director Guy Hamilton was given the
deciding vote and he too preferred Roger over Billington.

(396) Roger Moore was the first actor to shoot a second

gunbarrel intro. He had to do this because of an aspect ratio change.

(397) Kim Basinger had never seen a Bond film before when she was cast in Never Say Never Again. It was Sean Connery's wife who suggested her for the part.

(398) Roger Moore had a bout of shingles shooting The Spy Who Loved Me. Shingles is a viral infection that causes a painful rash. Moore had a puffy face at one point (during the briefing scene with George Baker) and so they had to shoot a scene over his shoulder and avoid close-ups.

(399) Roger Moore fractured a tooth and suffered from kidney stones when production began on Live and Let Die. He certainly wouldn't be the last Bond actor to suffer for his art!

(400) For the 360 degree Barrel Roll car stunt over the bendy bridge in The Man With The Golden Gun, the car had to be driven at 39.5 and 40.5 mph and the placement had to be within 2 inches or else it all would all have gone horribly wrong.

(401) Ian Fleming, like his famous fictional character, was very fond of gambling. 'I do like to gamble,' Fleming said to Playboy in 1964. "I play bridge for what might be called serious stakes. I like chemin de fer. I play at clubs here in London, private clubs. And I may go to Le Touquet, places like that on the Continent. I like to think that I am reasonably competent at the gaming tables – we all think so, I suppose – but still, I win as much as I lose, or a bit more. I like that, which I suppose demonstrates that I am not a true compulsive gambler.'

(402) 1983 was a unique year because it saw the release of an official EON Bond film in Octopussy and an unofficial Bond film in Never Say Never Again. Despite all the Battle of the Bonds headlines, Roger Moore and Sean Connery remained friends and even had dinner a few times while these films were in production. Octopussy won the box-office battle and

outgrossed Never Say Never Again.

(403) Maurice Binder said he had to throw out some of his most beautiful titles imagery involving scantily clad (or even nude) women because it was too risque and wouldn't get past censors.

(404) Some film rushes (basically footage that hasn't been edited) from Never Say Never Again were sent to the Octopussy production offices by mistake. EON were perfect gentlemen about this. They arranged for the rushes to be sent back and made sure no one viewed them.

(405) Ian Fleming was always dismayed if a critic was snooty about his books. He wanted to be taken seriously as a writer and hated it when people said the Bond books were potboilers.

(406) On average, Bond has a drink every 10 minutes, 53 seconds in the movies.

(407) Anita Ekberg was considered for the part of Honey Ryder.

(408) The character of Nigel Small-Fawcett in Never Say Never Again was a last minute invention of Dick Clement and Ian La Frenais to give the film more humour. Rowan Atkinson, who played the character, was completely unknown outside of Britain at the time. Atkinson is famous in many countries now for playing Mr Bean.

(409) At one point, Charles and Diana (obviously played by actors) were going to have a cameo at the end of The Living Daylights in the same fashion that Margaret and Dennis Thatcher featured at the end of For Your Eyes Only. Thankfully though this plan was axed and abandoned before it got very far (apparently an actor had been cast as Prince Charles before the plug was sensibly pulled on this idea).

(410) The end credits for The World Is Not Enough originally

featured a Scott Walker song. After negative feedback about this song in preview screenings they replaced it with a version of the Bond theme.

(411) Roger Ebert gave Live and Let Die a lukewarm review when it came out in 1973. 'Live and Let Die is the ninth James Bond picture, and not exactly the best. It has all the necessary girls, gimmicks, subterranean control rooms, uniformed goons and magic wristwatches it can hold, but it doesn't have the wit and it doesn't have the style of the best Bond movies. This may have something to do with the substitution of Roger Moore for Sean Connery as 007. Moore has the superficial attributes for the job: The urbanity, the quizzically raised eyebrow, the calm under fire and in bed. But Connery was always able to invest the role with a certain humour, a sense of its ridiculousness. Moore has been supplied with a lot of double entendres and double takes, but he doesn't seem to get the joke.' Years later, Ebert would say exactly the same thing when The Living Daylights came out and say that Timothy Dalton didn't get the joke. You could understand saying this about Dalton but not Roger Moore!

(412) M actor Bernard Lee passed away before production on For Your Eyes Only. As a mark of respect, Cubby Broccoli did not recast the part for the movie. This is why Bond is briefed by James Villiers as Bill Tanner in For Your Eyes Only.

(413) Four different versions of Licence To Kill were released worldwide with Britain and Europe getting the most watered down version (in that cuts were made to violent scenes). The death of Krest in the decompression chamber (where his head explodes!) was one scene that had to be trimmed.

(414) Desmond Llewelyn was delighted at the expanded role for Q in Licence To Kill and later said he made more money from this Bond picture than any of the others.

(415) Terence Young said he liked From Russia with Love best out of the Bond films he directed.

(416) Desmond Llewelyn said he enjoyed Alec McCowen's version of Q in Never Say Never Again and appreciated the fact that McCowen did his own thing with the part and didn't try to copy or spoof the EON version of Q.

(417) No Time To Die was the first film in the Bond series to have sequences shot with 65mm IMAX film cameras.

(418) In 1981, a new series of James Bond continuation novels written by John Gardner began. Gardner had Bond driving a Saab and Bond's gadgets are supplied by Ann Reilly - who is known as Q'ute.

(419) Daniel Craig had two teeth knocked out making Casino Royale, suffered a bad leg injury making Spectre, and broke his ankle on No Time To Die.

(420) For what it's worth, Licence To Kill has a higher Rotten Tomatoes rating than Quantum of Solace or Spectre and a higher rating than the last three Brosnan films. Of the Brosnan era, only Goldeneye outscores Licence To Kill on RT and that's only by 1%. And yet people write about Licence To Kill as if it was a critical dud!

(421) Jack O'Halloran (best known as the mute bearded Kryptonian villain Non in Superman II) turned down the part of Jaws.

(422) Ana de Armas's Michael Lo Lorma Alexandra dress in No Time To Die costs about $1200 in real life but it quickly sold out once images of her wearing the dress were revealed.

(423) A real tarantula was used in the movie Dr No. Glass was placed between Sean Connery and the spider so it would appear to be walking over him.

(424) Goldfinger was the first movie to feature a laser beam.

(425) The stunt co-ordinator Bob Simmons is the man you see in the early Bond film gunbarrels.

(426) Terence Young got Sean Connery a Saville Row suit for Dr No and told him to sleep in it! Young wanted Connery to feel like an expensive suit was like a second skin.

(427) Roger Moore was the first Bond actor not to wear a hat in his gunbarrel opening.

(428) Cubby Broccoli built the largest soundstage in the world at Pinewood to make The Spy Who Loved Me. A huge space was needed for the supertanker interiors.

(429) Stanley Kubrick secretly helped with the lighting for the supertanker scenes in The Spy Who Loved Me. Kubrick did this as a favour to Bond's production designer Ken Adam.

(430) In his memoir When the Snow Melts, Cubby Broccoli said that Michael Redgrave, David Niven, Trevor Howard, and James Fox were all names they considered for the part of James Bond in Dr No.

(431) Terence Young claimed that Sean Connery asked him to direct Never Say Never Again.

(432) If you watched all the James Bond films back to back it would take you over 50 hours to get through them.

(433) Tomorrow Never Dies rejected several theme songs before Sheryl Crow's theme was chosen. Saint Etienne, Marc Almond, Swan Lee, The Cardigans, Space, and Pulp all had Tomorrow Never Dies theme songs rejected. The Swan Lee song (in my humble opinion) was the best of this bunch.

(434) Cary Fukunaga was reported to be chasing the Oscar winning actress Lupita Nyong'o for a role in No time To Die but this did not transpire in the end. She simply wasn't available. It seems plausible that Nyong'o was pursued for the

role eventually taken by Lashana Lynch.

(435) Before Sam Mendes decided to return, Nicolas Winding Refn was offered the chance to direct Spectre but he wasn't interested.

(436) The friendship between director Terence Young and Sean Connery on the early Bond films is said to have mitigated the fact that Connery didn't like the producers very much.

(437) John Gardner's James Bond continuation novels might well have inspired sequences in the films - though EON never admitted this. For example, before The Living Daylights and Tomorrow Never Dies came out, Gardner's Bond had been involved in a cargo plane fight and also indulged in remote control car shenanigans.

(438) No Time To Die's title was revealed in the Futura Black font. This font has been used for the title sequences of television shows like The Love Boat and Prisoner: Cell Block H and was also used as the wordmark for the National Football League's Minnesota Vikings from 1982 to 2003.

(439) Timothy Dalton said that when The Living Daylights came out he secretly slipped into a New York cinema so he could watch it with an audience.

(440) The novel Dr No was based a pilot script Ian Fleming had written for a proposed NBC television series called Commander Jamaica.

(441) In Fleming's novel The Man With The Golden Gun, it suggested that homosexual men can't whistle!

(442) Hans Zimmer brought in former Smiths guitarist Johnny Marr to work on the music for No Time To Die with him. Hans Zimmer said he had known Barbara Broccoli for many years but he'd never been asked to a Bond film before. He telephoned Johnny Marr to ask if he thought they should

do the Bond music together and accept the job and Marr told him they should definitely do the Bond film.

(443) Production began on Goldfinger before From Russia with Love had even been released to cinemas. The producers were super confident (even at this early stage) that they had a winning formula.

(444) The scene where Bond resigns in Licence To Kill was shot at the Hemingway house in Florida. This explains Bond's "farewell to arms" line.

(445) The Daily Mail reported that No Time To Die was the most environmental Bond film ever made. 'Crew members were given reusable water bottles which they filled from taps, saving an estimated 230,000 single-use plastic water bottles. More than 11 tons of packaging waste was also recycled, while producers sent 30 tons of food waste and biodegradable packaging to 'anaerobic digestion', in which micro-organisms break down material, producing a gas that can be used to generate electricity. A further 1.6 tons of food was donated to feed the homeless through the City Harvest charity. Even Bond's beloved gas-guzzling Aston Martin hasn't escaped the green makeover. Craig will drive an electric Rapide E model. Only 155 of the £250,000 vehicles have been built.'

(446) Sean Connery's renegade Bond film Never Say Never Again was produced by Jack Schwartzman. Jack Schwartzman was so terrified of Sean Connery he tried to avoid him on the set (which obviously couldn't have been an easy task). Connery, never one to suffer fools, thought that Schwartzman was incompetent and so the relationship between the men was difficult to say the least.

(447) The Acrostar plane stunt which opens Octopussy was originally conceived for the Moonraker PTS.

(448) John Landis was one of many writers who had a crack at coming up with a story treatment for The Spy Who Loved Me

in the mid 1970s. Landis wanted to begin the PTS with Bond all bloodied and bruised. He thought it would make an arresting start to the film because Roger Moore was usually so impeccably dressed and unflappable.

(449) It was actually Sean Connery's wife who came up with the title Never Say Never Again.

(450) Frank Rich in Time gave Moonraker a very positive review when the film came out. 'Those who have held out on Bond movies over 17 years may not be convinced by Moonraker, but everyone else will be. With their rigid formulas and well-worn gags, these films have transcended fashion. Styles in Pop culture, sexual politics and international espionage have changed drastically since Ian Fleming invented his superhero, but the immaculately tailored, fun-loving British agent remains a jolly spokesman for the simple virtues of Western civilization. Not even Margaret Thatcher would dare consider slowing him down.'

(451) Teri Hatcher as Paris Carver was supposed to have a larger role in Tomorrow Never Dies but some of her scenes were axed after test screenings indicated her character wasn't especially memorable.

(452) Harry Saltzman wanted Paul McCartney's Live and Let Die theme to be recorded by a female artist but McCartney said they could only use it if him and his band did the song.

(453) According to Robert Sellers in the book When Harry Met Cubby, Broccoli & Saltzman considered dumping Roger Moore a week into the production of Live and Let Die and tried to get Sean Connery back.

(454) Cary Fukunaga said that the look of No Time To Die was designed as if it takes place in twilight. He wanted a moody sort of ambiance. Fukunaga said that his biggest influence was Casino Royale - which he felt was vastly superior to the three Daniel Craig films that followed.

(455) A View To A Kill was called A Panorama To Kill in Spain.

(456) When they had to find a new James Bond actor for Goldeneye, Jason Isaacs, Mark Frankel, Greg Wise, Colin Wells, Ralph Fiennes, Liam Neeson, Jeremy Northam, James Purefoy, Sean Bean, Paul McGann, and Nathaniel Parker were all names mulled over by EON. In the end they cast Pierce Brosnan.

(457) At the press conference for Bond 25 (later to become No Time To Die), there was no news on what the film would be called. Michael G Wilson said they often didn't have a title at the start of production on a Bond film and so this was hardly a new situation. That was debatable to say the least. Most Bond films have a title when they launch their first official press conference.

(458) EON wanted Denis Villeneuve to direct No Time To Die but he was too busy making Dune and ruled himself out of consideration.

(459) Back in 1979, Roger Moore suggested he would not come back after Moonraker but he ended up making three more Bond movies.

(460) Out of the Bond films he made, Sean Connery said From Russia with Love was his favourite.

(461) When Richard Kiel as Jaws bites into the steel cable with his teeth in Moonraker, the cable was really made of liquorice.

(462) There was a mishap on the set of No time To Die when a controlled explosion damaged the 007 Stage at Pinewood Studios and left a crew member with minor injuries. The stunt was for a scene where a fireball rips through a laboratory. The resulting explosion damaged part of the roof of the 007 stage and blasted off five huge panels from the outside of the building. The British Health and Safety Executive, according

to press reports, launched an investigation and gave the Bond 'bosses' a telling off.

(463) Kanaga in the film Live and Let Die is named after the real-life owner of the crocodile farm. The crew got the idea of using the crocodile farm in the movie when they stumbled across a sign that read - Trespassers Will Be Eaten.

(464) In the final scene Daniel Craig shot on No Time To Die he was, appropriately enough, wearing a tuxedo and disappearing from view in a cloud of smoke. At the conclusion of the final scene, director Cary Fukunaga gave a short speech to the crew that had all gathered. There was a round of applause. Daniel Craig gave a speech too but was teary eyed and couldn't remember what he wanted to say. Some of the crew went back to Daniel Craig's trailer and had some cocktails to mark the end of the production. A special wrap party was held at the Masons' Hall in central London. Daniel Craig then flew home to New York - where he now lives.

(465) Before shooting began on A View To A Kill, the 007 stage at Pinewood Studios burned down. Cunny Broccoli mulled this disaster over for a moment and then simply ordered a new one to be built!

(466) Charles Dance, who was one of the villains in For Your Eyes Only, later played Ian Fleming in a television movie called Goldeneye.

(467) Cary Fukunaga, in interviews for No Time To Die, talked about how he had an idea that the end of 2015's Spectre all took place in Bond's head while he was being tortured by Blofeld in that chair. The end of Spectre could be a fever dream and Bond could wake to find himself still in the chair. This would be like the classic 1890 short story An Occurrence at Owl Creek Bridge by Ambrose Bierce. Fukunaga was joking. One can't imagine that Sam Mendes would have been too thrilled to see the last act of Spectre written off as a bad dream!

(468) 400 tonnes of artificial snow was needed during the production of Spectre because it was mild in Austria and there wasn't enough real snow.

(469) The motorbike sequence in No Time To Die was suggested by Daniel Craig at the last minute as he felt the film was lacking one more big 'trailer' moment stunt. A modified Triumph Bonneville Scrambler 1200 and early prototypes of the Triumph Tiger 900 featured in the No Time To Die chase scenes. The motorbike stunt was performed by Paul "Fast Eddy" Edmondson - a former professional motorcycle enduro racer and a four-time World Enduro Champion. Edmondson had to hit an eight metre ramp at 60 mph to jump over a 22 metre wall.

(470) Dick Clement and Ian La Frenais, two legendary British sitcom writers, were hired by Sean Connery to polish the script for Never Say Never Again. Clement and La Frenais's script had the opening to the movie (where Connery's Bond is infiltrating a jungle mansion) playing out against the backdrop of a ticking clock to make it tense and exciting.

Clement and La Frenais were mortified when they watched the film and saw that the exciting opening sequence now had Lani Hall's soppy theme song over it rather than a ticking clock.

(471) Bonnie Tyler turned down the chance to sing the Never Say Never Again title song because she hated the song. "I really would die to do a James Bond song, you know? My heart wouldn't have been in it. I had to turn it down. Now how many people turn down a Bond song, I don't know. But I turned it down because I didn't like it. And I was proved right. It didn't appeal to me at all. So I turned it down. And that's the only regret that I have."

(472) Sean Connery once worked as a coffin polisher.

(473) Croatian actor Goran Visnjic, best known as Dr Luka

Kovac in US TV drama ER, auditioned to play James Bond in 2006's Casino Royale.

(474) A deleted scene in Licence To Kill had Bond sitting in his hotel room watching Franz Sanchez appear on television.

(475) Roger Moore is the oldest actor to be cast as Bond. Roger was 45 when he was cast in Live and Let Die. He looked much younger though.

(476) One of the awkward things about 2008's Quantum of Solace was that it created a crime syndicate known as the Quantum Organisation to essentially act as a replacement for SPECTRE. SPECTRE and Blofeld were unavailable to EON for many years because of Kevin McClory. The Quantum Organisation then became redundant two films later when SPECTRE and Blofeld returned to the series. The Quantum Organisation was a clumsy adjunct to the title Quantum of Solace - a genuine Fleming title that shouldn't have had to justify itself.

(477) It has been alleged that MGM wanted to cast Robert Redford as Bond after Sean Connery left for the second time but the chances of Redford accepting the role were close to zero. Redford was one of the biggest stars in Hollywood at the time so why would he have wanted to contract himself to Bond films when he had his pick of projects anyway?

(478) Daniel Craig said he (some time ago now) watched a rough cut of the much delayed No Time To Die in Soho and was happy with how it had turned out. Craig said he decided to watch the film alone so that he could absorb it fully and concentrate. There was no music score and the special effects hadn't been finished but Craig felt the film worked.

(479) When the Lotus comes out of the water onto the beach in The Spy Who Loved Me, the car was secretly pulled by a rope to achieve the effect of it driving out of the sea. The car they used wasn't watertight either so Roger Moore and Barbara

Bach got their feet wet shooting this scene.

(480) James Bond producer Michael G. Wilson has said it's very difficult to give Bond an impressive new gadget in an age when everyone has an iPhone in their pocket. It is exceptionally difficult now to give Bond a fancy new gizmo that will impress anyone in this age of high technology.

(481) The character of Hergerscheimer in Diamonds Are Forever is a joke by Tom Mankiewicz. It was based on the fact that whenever the director Guy Hamilton couldn't remember someone's name he would just call them Hergerscheimer.

(482) MGM wanted Sharon Stone to play Elektra King in The World Is Not Enough but they obviously didn't get their way on this.

(483) The late film critic Roger Ebert felt that Goldfinger was the movie which established the Bond formula. 'The Broccoli-Saltzman formula found its lasting form in the making of "Goldfinger." The outline was emerging in the first two films, and here it is complete. First, the title sequence, establishing Bond as a sex hound while linking him with a stunt sequence or a spectacular death. Then the summons by M, head of British Secret Service, and the briefing on a villain obsessed by global domination. The flirtation with Moneypenny. The demonstration by Q of new gimmicks invented especially for his next case. Then the introduction of the villain, his murderous and bizarre sidekick, and his female assistant/accomplice/mistress. Bond's discovery of the nature of the villain's evil scheme. Bond's capture and the certainty of death. Bond's seduction of the villain's woman. And so on, leading always to a final scene in which Bond is about to enjoy his victory reward: the sensuous fruits of his latest conquest.'

(484) Diana Rigg said she disliked the clothes she was given to wear in On Her Majesty's Secret Service. "I didn't like my Bond Girl outfits. The designer was a friend of the directors and I thought they were too boring and middle-aged for my

character."

(485) Roger Moore's daughter Deborah made a cameo in Die Another Day as a flight stewardess.

(486) Louis Jordan was in contention to play Hugo Drax in Moonraker. Jordan would later play the villain in Octopussy.

(487) Fifteen BMW 750s were destroyed during the production of Tomorrow Never Dies.

(488) The writer Tom Manciwiecz lobbied for Diana Ross to play Solitare in Live and Let Die. It is alleged that United Artists though were not comfortable at the thought of a black female lead in a Bond film (this was 1972 when times were, sadly, very different).

(489) The French composer Eric Serra supplied a rather eccentric score for the 1995 film Goldeneye. For reasons best known to himself, Serra seemed highly reluctant to use the Bond theme. The producers had to add the 007 theme to the big tank chase themselves.

(490) Timothy Dalton cut the size of Bond's wardrobe by about a third in comparison to the previous 007 films. He had firm ideas about what Bond should or shouldn't wear and how his lifestyle should be depicted. "Bond was never flash or ostentatious," said Dalton of the books. "In fact, he really wore a uniform, a dark suit, navy blue. He was very navy blue. He wasn't a wealthy man."

(491) Licence To Kill was called Private Revenge in Italy.

(492) In the Fleming novels, Bond's cigarettes are from Morlands of Grosvesnor street. They are made from a blend of Balkan and Turkish tobacco.

(493) Lois Maxwell said of her early impressions of Sean Connery - "I had first met Sean in Cubby's office back at the

beginning. He had that wonderful atmosphere of menace and moved, as Cubby said, like a panther. But he was still a poor young actor in rumpled corduroys who looked like he lived in a bedsit. By 1964, however, when we had the party at the Dorchester for the third film, Goldfinger, he was very much his own man."

(494) The Bond Novels have sold over 100 million copies across the world.

(495) Brigitte Millar was considered for the part of Madeline in Spectre. In the end she had the smaller part of Dr Vogel.

(496) Don McLaughlan, the head of public relations at Lotus Cars, used an ingenious but simple ploy to get the Lotus in the Bond films. He simply parked a prototype Lotus Esprit at Pinewood Studios! Someone from EON saw the car and the Lotus ended up in The Spy Who Loved Me.

(497) When Live and Let Die was released in 1973, Richard Schickel in Time Magazine felt the movie was somewhat troubling in its attitudes to race. "Why are all the blacks either stupid brutes or primitives deep into the occult and voodooism? Why is miscegenation so often used as a turn-on? Why do such questions even arise in what is supposed to be pure entertainment?"

(498) Moonraker has the most shameless product placement scene in the history of the movie franchise when the ambulance navigates the hill and we see nothing but billboards in the background.

(499) The Ian Fleming novels are quite notorious for their sadism. Ian Fleming loved a good torture sequence.

(500) In Christopher Wood's novelisation of the film The Spy Who Loved Me, the real name of Jaws is Zbigniew Krycsiwiki.

(501) John Glen said that the reason why the keel-hauling

scene from Fleming's Live and Let Die novel took so long to appear in the movie franchise is that they knew it would be a difficult and complex sequence to shoot.

(502) There was an awful lot of speculation that Bond 25 (No Time to Die) was going to be called Shatterhand in the media. This turned out to be nonsense.

(503) Vijay Amritraj, who played Vijay in Octopussy, was a professional tennis player (which would explain the tennis sight gags in Octopussy). Amritraj was a friend of Cubby Broccoli and simply asked Cubby if he could be in a Bond film.

(504) Desmond Llewelyn said that it was Guy Hamilton more than anyone who informed the character of Q. When they made Goldfinger, Hamilton told Llewelyn that Q should be irritated by Bond because 007 is the man who always destroys all of Q's equipment and gadgets!

(505) Those who worked on Never Say Never Again say that Kim Basinger was very unhappy during the production because she didn't get with the director Irvin Kershner and found her part to be poorly written and largely decorative.

(506) The biggest surprise in the cast of Licence To Kill was the return of David Hedison as Felix Leiter - a role he had previously played in Live and Let Die alongside Roger Moore in 1973. At 61, Hedison was nearly twenty years older than Timothy Dalton so this casting was somewhat eccentric to say the least. No one was more surprised than Hedison himself at his return. Hedison had bumped into Cubby and Dana Broccoli at the Bistro Gardens in Beverly Hills and several weeks later got a call from John Glen inviting him to be in the film. Hedison was happy to accept this unexpected chance to be in a James Bond film again.

(507) Ian Fleming once said - 'Spies are trained to keep their mouths shut and they don't often lose the habit. That's why true spy stories are extremely rare, and personally I have never

seen one in print that completely rang true. Even in fiction, there is very little good spy literature. There is something in the subject that leads to exaggeration, and the literary framework of 'a beginning and a middle and an end' doesn't belong to good spy writing, which should be full of loose ends and drabness and ultimate despair. Perhaps only Somerset Maugham and Graham Greene and Eric Ambler have caught the squalor and greyness of the Secret Service.'

(508) Dougray Scott claims that the Bond producers spoke to him about becoming Bond before Pierce Brosnan returned for Die Another Day.

(509) When he first acquired his Thunderball movie rights, Kevin McClory is said to have approached Laurence Harvey to play James Bond. Richard Burton was his first choice though.

(510) Regarding the criticism that Denise Richards did not make a tremendously plausible nuclear scientist in The World Is Not Enough, the director Michael Apted said - "I wanted Denise for the role because she has a great look and is a terrific, serious actress, but if you don't believe it, you don't believe it. That's show business. It's not that well developed a role, and it can't be. I'm not doing Chekhov. It's part of the high wire of the film that you have to deliver babes. And Denise is a terrific babe. I hope I didn't hang her out to dry. I think she did very well, but she did have a bit less to work with than Sophie Marceau."

(511) Rick Sylvester was the man who performed the incredible mountain ski jump in the PTS of The Spy Who Loved. How did this stunt come to be? "For a very long time I thought the best part of the whole thing was the phone call," said Sylvester, telling the story. "I picked up the receiver to hear, "This is London calling. I'm Cubby Broccoli, like the vegetable [that's how he introduced himself], the producer of the Bond films ... we're wondering if you'd be interested in performing your jump in the next Bond film." The "jump" he was referring to was what I then called a ski parachute jump, featured in a

Canadian Club Whisky ad that was circulating at the time.
Years before Mountain Dew and Red Bull, Canadian Club ran
print ads based around an adventure motif. Cubby's son-in-
law Michael Wilson had seen the ad, which gave them the idea
of adding it to the film. It wasn't in Ian Fleming's book. The
only one of his Bond novels that had a ski sequence was On
Her Majesty's Secret Service with one-time Bond George
Lazenby.

For the movie, I recommended Mt. Asgard for the jump
sequence to the Bond team. It's a double summited peak,
6,600 feet in elevation, 25 miles north of the Arctic Circle on
Canada's Baffin Island. It's a spectacular land, somewhat
resembling multitudes of Yosemite Valleys but before the Ice
Age departed. At Asgard I would have no worry of tree
encounters, the timber line petering out something like 800
miles to the south. The stunt, filmed during the brief Arctic
summer, reputedly cost around a quarter of a million dollars.
The original budget for the film was $14 million but ultimately
came in around $21 million. Either way, that stunt, the most
expensive ever at that point, represented a huge chunk of the
entire budget. And this despite the fact that it didn't involve
constructing any elaborate and expensive sets. It wasn't even
as long as it seemed since the cameras were somewhat over
cranked, i.e. it was shot partially in slow motion. Actually, I
always thought gravity should have gotten an equal credit. And
there was another factor, one I'd mentioned to no one. I was
getting scared. The old thing about pushing it, daring the devil,
doing another jump, and this time not just for adventure but
for filthy lucre, had begun haunting me. Awakening day after
day to poor weather, I was experiencing melancholic thoughts
like "one more day of life." All this made the scramble to get to
the shoot an unpleasant surprise.

As we flew to the film site, it was clear that the fellows on the
scouting flight had not lied. It certainly wasn't sunny but it
also wasn't raining or snowing. Clouds swirled about Asgard
creating an ethereal effect. The glacier was obscured in what
looked like cotton candy. Everyone disembarked and hurriedly

began preparing what they had to do. I clipped into my skis, tied into a rope, and got belayed by Rob as I sideslipped the short, steep-ish slope to the edge to smooth out the snow since it bore a bit of crust — never my favored condition. This is apparent in the film to viewers who are observant. I donned my chute and checked to make sure everything was in order. Throughout all the hubbub around me as everyone set up, I was not all that happy. Finally, John Glen, the film editor, asked if I was ready. I couldn't come up with a reason to answer in the negative, so I replied yes. Over his radio he gave the "cameras rolling" instruction and then the nod to me to begin. I kicked off and a few seconds later dropped my poles just before the edge.

Once into space I got rid of the skis, but then experienced some trouble getting stable. Skydivers wear bulky jumpsuits and normal foot apparel. This helps compress the air beneath them which enables them to have the control to enact various positions and manoeuvrers, but during my ski BASE jumps I was clad in tight ski clothing and heavy ski boots. That combination, along with my relative inexperience in skydiving had affected my ability to get into the proper arched-back spread-eagle body position before pulling the ripcord. It's why I fell so far on the first El Cap jump before getting the chute deployed. The next two jumps saw vast improvement, but now it appeared I'd regressed. Finally, I felt I was close enough to a stable position and I pulled. A chute in the design of the British Union Jack flag opened beautifully. Except one of the skis struck the chute — well, nothing's perfect. I sailed down and landed nicely on the glacier, no trees to worry about."

(512) The actor Eric Braeden (best known now for daytime dramas and soaps) said that he could have been James Bond were it not for his German nationality. "Sean Connery had quit the franchise. The producer Cubby Broccoli took me to lunch to talk about my playing James Bond. It was a nice lunch, but he asked if I had a British passport. I said, "No, I have a German passport." An hour later, my agent was calling to give me Broccoli's verdict: No one who was not a member of the

British Commonwealth would ever play James Bond."

(513) Skyfall grossed $1.109 billion from a $150 million budget.

(514) Quantum of Solace was called A Grain of Comfort in Croatia.

(515) Monica Bellucci is the oldest ever Bond Girl. She was 50 when she appeared in Spectre.

(516) Sean Connery once did an interview in the late 1970s in which he said he'd recently gone to the cinema to watch Roger Moore in Moonraker. It probably won't come as a huge surprise to learn that Connery thought the film was rather silly.

(517) The mansion belonging to Sanchez in the movie Licence To Kill was owned by friends of Cubby Broccoli. In return for a donation to a charity of their choice, Broccoli was given permission to use the house in the film.

(518) When people do their Bond film rankings, A View To A Kill tends to rank near the bottom. The film had its fans though. John Brosnan in Starburst called it the best of the Roger Moore Bonds. The Canadian critic Lawrence O'Toole wrote of A View To A Kill - 'Of all the modern formulas in the movie industry, the James Bond series is among the most pleasurable and durable. Lavish with their budgets, the producers also bring a great deal of craft, wit and a sense of fun to the films. Agent 007 is like an old friend who an audience meets for drinks every two years or so; he regales them with tall tales, winking all the time. The 14th and newest Bond epic, A View to a Kill, is an especially satisfying encounter. Opening with a breathtaking ski chase in Siberia, A View to a Kill is the fastest Bond picture yet. Its pace has the precision of a Swiss watch and the momentum of a greyhound on the track. There is a spectacular chase up and down the Eiffel Tower and through Paris streets, which Bond finishes in

a severed car on just two wheels. But none of the action prepares the viewer for the heart-stopping climax with Zorin's dirigible tangled in the cables on top of San Francisco's Golden Gate Bridge.'

(519) Bond special effects and models expert Derek Meddings said of his time on the movies - "Wherever we went, Cubby would bestow great luxury upon us. As heads of departments we were sent on location recces and put in the best hotels. We flew first class, it was luxury. We went from Los Angeles down to Rio, out to the Belize jungle. They were great days. It spoils you in the end, because you find that you can't afford to stay in these hotels and you can't afford to fly first class, unless Cubby Broccoli is paying..."

(520) Bruce Feirstein, who wrote on the movie Tomorrow Never Dies, said he was disappointed by how the film turned out. "I personally did not want all of the running and shooting in the film. I had a different kind of conception for the character of Eliot Carver. I wanted him to be much more like Goldfinger. I have a background in journalism, where I have at one time or another worked for all the moguls. I didn`t see this as being a character who was surrounded by eighteen guys in black camo-gear, carrying uzis or whatever. I saw him as a guy being surrounded by eighteen guys with briefcases. That was lost."

(521) Tom Mankiewicz said that Catherine Deneuve wanted the part of Anya Amasova in the Spy Who Loved Me but negotiations broke down because cubby Broccoli wasn't willing to pay the $250,000 she wanted to star in the film.

(522) The Walther PPK was first used by the German police in 1931.

(523) The Seven Mile Bridge, where Sanchez escapes in Licence To Kill after the police van crashes into the sea, was later used in the 1994 James Cameron spy adventure film True Lies.

(524) The first Michael France draft of the Goldeneye script begins with a PTS action sequence involving a futuristic train.

(525) The only Bond actor who seems to have exerted a creative control over the franchise is Daniel Craig. Craig practically became a co-producer on his movies and enjoyed considerable input into the scripts, choice of writers, choice of director, and even the artist to do the theme song. Timothy Dalton and Pierce Brosnan could only dream of such influence.

(526) Pinewood Studios was used to depict Cuba in parts of No Time To Die. A number of elaborate and impressive Havana street sets were built at Pinewood.

(527) The first ever scene Pierce Brosnan shot as James Bond was driving the Aston Martin in Monte Carlo for Goldeneye.

(528) Harry Saltzman was said to be obsessed with gadgets - much more so than Cubby Broccoli. So the tradition of gadgets in Bond films probably stems from Harry Saltzman.

(529) Bernard Lee wasn't in the best of health when they made Live and Let Die. The producers apparently had Kenneth More lined up as a replacement M.

(530) The moon buggy in Diamonds Are Forever kept breaking down during the chase sequence because it wasn't designed for rocky desert terrain.

(531) The fictional Republic of Isthmus in Licence To Kill is based on Panama.

(532) Daniel Craig was 51 when No Time To Die finished shooting. Only Roger Moore had been older while making an EON Bond film. Pierce Brosnan was 49 when he made his last film. Timothy Dalton was 44. Sean Connery was 40 when he shot his 'official' swansong Diamonds Are Forever. George

Lazenby was 30 when he made his one and only Bond film.

(533) In the 1990s there were stories that a new version of Never Say Never Again was going to be released on laserdisc with a new music score and much deleted footage put back in. Most Bond fans would pay money to watch that.

(534) Regarding his descriptive passages about food in the Bond novels, Fleming wrote - 'I have never understood why people in books have to eat such sketchy and indifferent meals. English heroes seem to live on cups of tea and glasses of beer, and when they do get a square meal we never hear what it consists of. Personally, I am not a gourmet and I abhor food-and-winemanship. My favourite food is scrambled eggs. In the original typescript of Live and Let Die, James Bond consumed scrambled eggs so often that a perceptive proof-reader suggested that this rigid pattern of life must be becoming a security risk for Bond. If he was being followed, his tail would only have to go into restaurants and say "Was there a man here eating scrambled eggs?" to know whether he was on the right track or not. So I had to go through the book changing the menus.'

(535) It was Sean Connery who chose Edward Fox to play M in Never Say Never Again. Fox plays M as a priggish upper-class bureaucrat who doesn't seem to like Bond very much.

(536) In the Brosnan movie The World Is Not Enough, MI6 had an emergency headquarters in Scotland. You can see a portrait of Bernard Lee as M on the wall of this HQ.

(537) In the original script for Tomorrow Never Dies, the henchman Stamper is impervious to pain. This was later transplanted to the villain Renard in The World Is Not Enough.

(538) Helen Mirren was considered for the part of Solitaire in Live and Let Die. Jane Seymour played this part in the end.

(539) Sean Connery's tattoos had to be covered up when he played Bond in the EON films. You can see them in Never Say Never Again though.

(540) The PTS of Octopussy, though set in Cuba, was actually shot at RAF Northolt in London. They simply added a few fake palm trees.

(541) The American bodybuilder and actor Steve Reeves said he turned down the part of James Bond in Dr No. Reeves claimed that the money they offered him was an insult.

(542) Britt Ekland, who played Mary Goodnight in The Man with the Golden Gun, said that Cubby Broccoli thought she was too thin so before shooting began he took her to a lot of Italian restaurants to try and fatten her up and gain a few more curves.

(543) In an interview many years after Bond, Sean Connery said that no one had the faintest idea if Dr No was going to become a success when they were making it. "Everyone who said that the first one was going to be a success is a liar because they didn't know. The film costs less than a million dollars. They didn't make one immediately afterwards because they still weren't sure. Everybody forgets that. Believe me, nobody could have foreseen that all these years later, we'd be sitting here discussing James Bond."

(544) James Bond's kill count in the film Quantum of Solace is estimated to be sixteen victims.

(545) The Japanese government would only allow the Bond team to shoot in Japan for You Only Live Twice if Japanese actresses were cast in leading roles.

(546) The Prince and Princess of Wales visited the production of The Living Daylights at Pinewood in 1986 and Diana famously got to smash a prop bottle over Charles' head.

(547) Martin Grace was the stunt double for Richard Kiel's Jaws in the movies. To depict the steel teeth of Jaws, Grace put tin foil wrapped orange peel in his mouth!

(548) Roger Moore actually became a very accomplished skier after moving to Switzerland in the 1970s. Even so, he wasn't allowed to ski in the James Bond films for insurance and safety reasons.

(549) Bond model miniature maestro Derek Meddings said it was tricky to make the Liparus tanker model in The Spy who Loved Me seem convincing.

"The reason we built it so large was because we had to deal with submarines in the same shots. Water is always a problem when you're dealing with miniatures because you just can't scale it, you've got to be clever enough to shoot it the right way at a very high speed - the secret is to make certain you don't create a splash which is, of course, going to produce big globules of water on the screen and immediately give the game away. Even though our tanker was sixty-three feet long, it would only create a bow wave and wash that was in scale with a sixty-three-foot launch, which is nothing like what a supertanker with its vast displacement of water would create. Only the aft section was actually built like a boat, the rest was like a catamaran built on two floats. We had a huge 175 horsepower marlin engine in it which gave us a terrific wake though, of course, nothing near a real tankers.2

(550) Skyfall was the first Bond film to gross a billion dollars. This was slightly misleading though because 1965's Thunderball would have made over a billion dollars in 2012 money.

(551) The black actress Gloria Hendry (who plays Rosie) was removed from the promotional art for Live and Let Die in apartheid South Africa.

(552) Believe it or not, Pierce Brosnan is both the lightest and

heaviest person to play Bond. He was very slender in Goldeneye but bulked up for Tomorrow Never Dies.

(553) It was sometimes said that Diana Rigg hated George Lazenby so much she ate garlic before their love scenes in OHMSS. This is not actually true. Rigg apparently merely joked to Lazenby in the canteen one day about having garlic for lunch.

(554) Steven Spielberg was desperate to direct a Bond film in the 1970s and telephoned Cubby Broccoli to offer his services. Roger Moore said that Spielberg made his Bond pitch after his classic television movie Duel came out. Moore was sold on Spielberg but Cubby though wasn't convinced that this very young director (who had mostly worked in television at the time directing episodes of shows like Columbo and Night Gallery) was the best person to put in charge of a huge production like Bond. After the astonishing success of Jaws (which more or less invented the summer blockbuster), Spielberg became unrealistic as an option for EON because he would be too expensive.

(555) Little Nellie, the Gyrocopter in You Only Live Twice, was built and flown by Wing Commander Ken Wallis.

(556) Richard Kiel attributed his Spy Who Loved Me casting as Jaws to a television show called Barbary Coast. Kiel said that a casting director saw him in the show and suggested him to the Bond people.

(557) A sequence was shot for The Living Daylights where Bond (while in Tangiers) escapes from some baddies by sliding down some wires on a rug (thus making it appear as if he is on a magic carpet) and then hops on the back of a motorcycle. This 'flying carpet' sequence was left on the cutting room floor because it felt too Roger Moorish for the Timothy Dalton era. The director John Glen was also unhappy at the way the rug looked.

(558) When the media speculate who the next Bond might be they sometimes throw a few actresses into the mix as if James Bond is suddenly going to become Jane Bond. This recent speculation about a gender switch was probably inspired by Jodie Whittaker becoming the first female lead in Doctor Who. However, the Doctor is a regenerating alien. There is a plausible (as far as a sci-fi show can be plausible) explanation for why the Doctor (having previously been male) is now a woman. There is no such explanation for why James Bond should suddenly become a woman. Barbara Broccoli shot this speculation down in flames when she said that Bond would always be a man and she would prefer that new interesting roles for women were created rather than male characters become female.

(559) Tom Mankiewicz (who wrote the script) felt that Jane Seymour was miscast as Solitare in Live and Let Die. Mankiewicz felt that Seymour looked far too young and innocent and this made it seem as if Bond was taking advantage of her.

(560) Aston Martin was founded in a small London workshop in 1913 by the engineer Robert Bamford and the car enthusiast Lionel Martin.

(561) Robert Brown got the part of M on the suggestion of Roger Moore.

(562) The Diamonds Are Forever moon buggy was later rescued from a muddy field and restored by Graham Rye of 007 Magazine. It was then sold to Planet Hollywood.

(563) Even adjusted for inflation, Sean Connery is the lowest paid Bond actor after George Lazenby. In today's money, Connery earned about $3.5 million per Bond film. By way of contrast, Daniel Craig was paid an average of around $10 million per Bond film. Roger Moore was paid double Sean's salary on his Bond films. By far the worst paid Bond actor is George Lazenby. Adjusted for inflation in today's money,

Lazenby was paid about $400,000 for On Her Majesty's Secret Service. This made his decision to walk away from Bond after one film even more crazy. He should have done a couple more Bond films and then at least he could have walked away with a few million in the bank!

(564) Roger Ebert gave Connery's return in Diamonds Are Forever a fairly positive review in 1971 - 'The cultists like the early James Bond movies best, but I dunno. They may have been more tightly directed films, but they didn't understand the Bond mythos as fully as "Goldfinger" and "Diamonds Are Forever." We see different movies for different reasons, and Diamonds Are Forever is great at doing the things we see a James Bond movie for. Not the least of these is the presence of Sean Connery, who was born to the role: dry, unflappable (even while trapped in a coffin at a crematorium), with a mouth that does as many kinds of sly grins as there are lascivious possibilities in the universe. There's something about his detachment from danger that props up the whole Bond apparatus, insulating it from the total ridiculousness only an inch away.

In Diamonds Are Forever, for example, Bond finds himself driving a moon buggy (antennae wildly revolving and robot arms flapping) while being chased across a desert -- never mind why. The buggy looks comical, but Connery does not; he is completely at home, as we know by now, with every form of transportation. Later, after outsmarting five Las Vegas squad cars in a lovely chase scene, he nonchalantly flips his Mustang up on two wheels to elude the sixth. But not a sign of a smile. There is an exhilaration in the way he does it, even more than in the stunt itself. The plot of Diamonds Are Forever is as complicated as possible. That's necessary in order to have somebody left after nine dozen bad guys have been killed. It has been claimed that the plot is too complicated to describe, but I think I could if I wanted to. I can't imagine why anyone would want to, though. The point in a Bond adventure is the moment, the surface, what's happening now. The less time wasted on plot, the better.'

(565) Peter Hunt (director of OHMSS) said that Sean Connery approached him about directing Never Say Never Again. Hunt said he he couldn't accept the offer because he would have felt like a 'traitor' to EON and Cubby Broccoli.

(566) As part of his deal to return as Bond in Diamonds are Forever, United Artists agreed to fund any two films of Sean Connery's choice. The disturbing 1973 crime drama The Offence (in which Connery well and truly sheds his James Bond image) was the only picture that resulted from this deal though. Connery had planned the other film to be an adaptation of Macbeth but this never got made in the end.

(567) Before George Lazenby quite the Bond franchise after one movie, Richard Maibaum wrote a treatment for Diamonds are Forever in which Bond seeks revenge on Blofeld for the murder of his wife in On Her Majesty's Secret Service. Irma Bunt and Marc Ange Draco returned in the treatment. Cubby Broccoli was said to have disliked the story though and when Lazenby vacated the role of 007 the notion of doing a direct sequel to On Her Majesty's Secret Service lost a lot of its currency anyway.

(568) No Time To Die became the first number one single in the UK for Billie Eilish.

(569) Live and Let Die is the only Bond film that overtly leans into the horror genre.

(570) If Cubby Broccoli didn't like a script he would ask for more 'bumps' to be added. This was essentially his code for more Bondian staples. "Where are the bumps?" he would ask if the story wasn't sufficiently drenched in enough cinematic 007 residue for his liking.

(571) When Bond's Lotus comes out of the sea onto a beach in The Spy Who Loved Me, Bond hands a fish to a bemused onlooker before he drives off. Cubby Broccoli didn't like the

fish joke (he wondered how a fish would get in a waterproof underwater car!) and wanted it removed but Lewis Gilbert and Roger Moore both loved it and persuaded Cubby to let it remain the film.

(572) In 1989, while promoting Licence To Kill, Timothy Dalton said - "I think Roger was fine as Bond but the films had become too much techno-pop and had lost track of their sense of story. I mean, every film seemed to have a villain who had to rule or destroy the world. If you want to believe in the fantasy on screen, then you have to believe in the characters and use them as a stepping-stone to lead you into this fantasy world. That's a demand I made, and Albert Broccoli agreed with me."

(573) The construction site chase which begins Casino Royale took three weeks to shoot.

(574) Michael Praed, star of the television show Robin of Sherwood, said he did a James Bond audition for The Living Daylights.

(575) Pierce Brosnan badly injured his knee shooting the PTS of Die Another Day. It seems that none of the Bond actors have managed to avoid getting injured. It comes with the job.

(576) For many years Fleming's first James Bond novel Casino Royale eluded Eon Productions. The rights used to be held by the film producer Charles Feldman. Feldman, for reasons best known to himself, made a film version of Casino Royale in 1967 as an overblown comedy spoof. Woody Allen, one of the stars of the film, later called Feldman's Casino Royale "an unredeemingly moronic enterprise."

(577) Orson Welles was considered for the part of Auric Goldfinger but he wanted too much money to play the part.

(578) You Only Live Twice grossed $111.6 million on a budget of $10.3 million.

(579) Breakfast is the favourite meal of the day for Fleming's literary Bond and usually consists of scrambled eggs, bacon, toast, coffee, marmalade, and chilled orange juice.

(580) It is often claimed that Casino Royale (2006) was the first Bond film to feature rain. However, there appear to be a few splats of rain in On Her Majesty's Secret Service.

(581) Gayle Hunnicutt was the original choice to play Solitaire in Live and Let Die but had to pull out when she became pregnant.

(582) Madeline Smith was only paid £100 to play Miss Caruso in Live and Let Die. "It was a tiny amount. You hardly got anything at all in those days. But I was 23, and it was a wonderful experience. I absolutely loved Roger Moore. I could not believe it when I got the part. I never even auditioned for it. I had been in an episode of The Persuaders, which Roger had directed, and unbeknown to me, he suggested me for the part."

(583) Gerard Butler has a small part in Tomorrow Never Dies as a British sailor. Butler was later mentioned a lot in the media as a potential candidate to replace Brosnan as 007 but he wasn't a serious contender for Casino Royale in the end.

(584) Spectre grossed $880.7 million from a $250 million budget.

(585) Coming up with new and original stunts is an almost impossible task after 25 Bond films - not to mention all the other action films that have stolen Bond's thunder and come up with Bond style stunts themselves. Bond has been in car chases, ski chases, motorbike chases, Bobsleigh chases, helicopter chases, speedboat chases. He's fallen out of an aeroplance without a parachute, had laser battles in space, been winched out of a helicopter, had fights in cargo planes, flipped a car on its side, driven a tank, had fistfights on trains, flown a jet fighter, bungee jumped off a dam, done a HALO

jump, skied off a mountain, and (lest we forget) parasurfed a glacier. Bond has had a car chase on ice, a fight on top of a cable car, driven a car underwater, fought in a battle on an oil rig, a battle in Fort Knox, a battle in a volcano. Bond has flown in a jetpack, jumped over alligators, motorbiked over a helicopter, flown a gyrocopter, driven a tanker truck. Over the course of 25 films James Bond has done literally everything it is possible to do in an action film.

(586) Bond is seen driving a blue Land Rover Series III in No Time To Die. This Land Rover had been seen in the Bond series before when it featured in the pre-title sequence on Gibraltar for The Living Daylights.

(587) Fleming's literary Bond has a nine handicap at golf.

(588) Geoffry Holder, who plays Baron Samedi in Live and Let Die, had a fear of snakes. Making this snake festooned movie was no picnic for him.

(589) The film Moonraker is often tagged as EON's attempt to latch onto the Star Wars craze but you could argue that the movie is more influenced by Kubrick's 2001 than Star Wars.

(590) There was an attempt to cast Orson Welles as Blofeld in Never Say Never Again.

(591) Peter Purves, later best known as a presenter on the BBC children's magazine show Blue Peter, said he auditioned for the part of James Bond when Sean Connery left after You Only Live Twice.

(592) Octopussy was called 007 Against the Deadly Girls in Mexico.

(593) Honour Blackman quit her role as Cathy Gale in the television show The Avengers so she could be in Goldfinger.

(594) Cubby Broccoli said that Dr No director Terence Young

was dismayed when he learned that they'd cast Sean Connery as Bond. Young thought that Connery was going to be a disaster.

(595) The German actress Julia Bremermann was director Roger Spottiswoode's choice to play Paris Carver in Tomorrow Never Dies but he obviously didn't get his way on this.

(596) Retrospectives which have dismissed the Timothy Dalton era as a misfire or failure tend to forget that both Dalton and The Living Daylights were well received in 1987. The Living Daylights outgrossed the previous three Roger Moore films. Licence To Kill suffered in the United States because of a penny pinching marketing campaign by MGM. It still did well around the world though. Were it not for studio litigation Dalton would have made at least four films.

(597) After he quite the Bond franchise, George Lazenby took some acting lessons in an attempt to boost his career. It didn't really make much difference.

(598) Believe it or not, despite the Miami and Fort Knox scenes, Sean Connery didn't shoot anything in the United States for Goldfinger. Most of this stuff was done in England.

(599) Harry Saltzman was the person who came up with the idea of having a pre-credit sequence in the Bond films.

(600) The shark attack on Leiter in Licence To Kill was taken from Fleming's Live and Let Die novel.

(601) It is often reported that Ian Fleming gave James Bond some Scottish ancestry as a tribute to Sean Connery but this is not true. Fleming decided to give Bond Scottish ancestry before Sean Connery and the movies came along.

(602) Hugh Jackman said he was approached about playing James Bond around the time that X-Men 2 was entering production. Jackman told the Bond people that he was simply

too busy and bound up in contracts to pursue the role.

(603) Daniel Craig, famously, made some ill-advised off the cuff comments at the end of the Spectre shoot when he said he would rather 'slash his own wrists' than make another Bond film. This was clearly a stupid (not to mention offensive) thing to say and a consequence of being tired and sore after an exhausting six month shoot. Craig, in mitigation for his comments, would later say that he shot Spectre in constant pain because of a leg injury he suffered during the production. He'd also spent close to a year away from home and his family completing his commitments to the film (a Bond actor is obviously required to do extensive stunt training before the film and extensive publicity to promote the film after it is completed).

(604) Although the scene with Madeline Smith's Miss Caruso opens Live and Let Die, it was actually the last scene to be shot during the production.

(605) Sean Connery offered the director's chair on Never Say Never Again to Richard Donner but Donner wasn't interested and passed.

(606) During the production of Moonraker in Paris, the French actress Carole Bouquet visited the set. Bouquet obviously made a big impression on Cubby Broccoli because he cast her in the next movie - For Your Eyes Only.

(607) In the United States, Licence To Kill opened the same week as the sleeper hit When Harry Met Sally.

(608) Mel Gibson said that he turned down James Bond twice because the part didn't interest him. Tom Mankiewicz, writer on some Bond films for Cubby Brocoli, disputed this though and said it was Cubby Broccoli who didn't want Gibson and not the other way around. According to Mankiewicz, Cubby felt Gibson was too famous and they would end up making a Mel Gibson movie rather than a James Bond movie. Cubby is

also alleged to have felt that the 5'9 Gibson was far too short to play James Bond. "Cubby had a thing about tall people," said Mankiewicz. "Bond had to be tall, and Mel Gibson was too short."

(609) Steven Seagal was the fight choreographer on Never say Never Again. He broke Sean Connery's wrist when they were training for a fight scene.

(610) Peter Jackson was in contention to direct The World Is Not Enough. It is alleged that he dropped out of contention after Barbara Broccoli screened his film The Frighteners and absolutely hated it.

(611) No Time to Die features a glider sequence as one of its major setpieces. The plane used is a (Fictional Glider) & Boeing C-17A Globemaster III. The glider has unfolding wings.

(612) Sean Connery injured his back shooting the scenes where Bond fights with Oddjob inside Fort Knox in Goldfinger.

(613) In the moon buggy sequence in Diamonds Are Forever, you can clearly see one of the wheels coming loose and then bouncing out of the frame.

(614) The gunbarrel opening for George Lazenby is quite novel because Lazenby goes down on one knee when he fires at the screen. The director Peter Hunt said he never liked this gunbarrel much.

(615) James Horner was supposed to score Never Say Never Again but was passed over for Michael Legrand. This is a shame because Horner was fantastic and Legrand's score isn't the best.

(616) The Bond franchise is one of the few examples of a huge mainstream movie where it doesn't really matter how famous the leading man is. No one knew Sean Connery from Adam

when he was cast as Bond. Daniel Craig was hardly a household name when he got the part. Pierce Brosnan was making television movies when he was cast as Bond. The only actor who had a reasonably high profile going into Bond was Roger Moore - thanks to his television shows The Saint and The Persuaders. Roger was most definitely not a film star though at the time and had no track record to speak of when it came to opening a movie with his mere presence.

(617) John Gardner wrote the novelisation of Licence To Kill and had a dreadful time trying to tie the story in with the continuity of the Fleming novels (where Leiter suffered an identical shark attack in Live and Let Die). In the end Gardner rather brushed over the return of Milton Krest (from The Hildebrand Rarity) and had the shark attacking Leiter's false leg from the previous attack! The Felix Leiter in the Gardner continuity must rank as one of the unluckiest people in history to experience two identical shark attacks!

(618) In the period between Thunderball and You Only Live Twice, Sean Connery did an interview in which he said - "The Bond pictures have become like comic strips dependent on bigger and better gimmicks. That's all that sustains them. There are even dolls with spikes that protrude from their shoes. It's a lot of rubbish."

(619) Adjusted for inflation, Thunderball is the 28th biggest grossing film of all time.

(620) It is never really entirely clear in the Bond series if Robert Brown's M is supposed to be the same character as Bernard Lee's M.

(621) No Time To Die's Ana de Armas is the first Cuban 'Bond Girl'. It was speculated that she was cast in the film by Daniel Craig because they had recently appeared in Knives Out together. However, it later came to light that Ana de Armas had met Barbara Broccoli several years ago and Broccoli had always liked the idea of the actress appearing in a Bond film

one day.

(622) Stana Katic was considered for the part of Strawberry Fields in Quantum of Solace.

(623) After Ian Fleming's death, a number of authors wrote James Bond continuation novels with varying degrees of success. Many Bond fans think the best of these books is Colonel Sun by Kingsley Amis (writing as Robert Markham).

(624) Lewis Collins, star of the action show The Professionals on television, was one of the post popular 007 candidates to replace Roger Moore in the 1980s. Sadly though for Lewis Collins, Cubby Broccoli was not so keen. "I was in Cubby Broccoli's office for five minutes," said Collins of his all too brief James Bond interview, "but it was really over for me in seconds. I have heard since that he doesn't like me. That's unfair. I think he's really shut the door on me. He found me too aggressive. If Cubby couldn't see I was being self-protective I don't have faith in his judgment."

(625) A View To A Kill begins with a disclaimer. The producers wanted to make sure no one confused Zorin with a real life company called the Zoran Corporation.

(626) The World Is Not Enough grossed $362 million from a $135 million budget.

(627) Ian Fleming's court case with Kevin McClory is believed to have been a contributing factor in his death. The stress clearly wasn't very good for him. Fleming was only 55 when he died but he wasn't the healthiest person in the world. He smoked like a chimney and drank too much.

(628) On designing the volcano set in You Only Live Twice, Ken Adam said - "We had the idea when we were scouting for locations in Japan. I showed some sketches to Cubby Broccoli and he said, 'That's quite a good idea, how much is it going to cost?' I said, 'I have no idea.' He said, 'If I give you a million

dollars, will you do it?' And I said, 'I'll do it.' Although I had no idea if it was possible. The height of the volcano crater lake from the floor of the set was 120 feet, the crater lake diameter was between 60 and 70 feet and I built it on an incline so you could see the whole circle. The diameter of the interior was about 400 feet so it was a huge structure. There were lots of problems, the pressure that the film would be on release in five months' time and the people who lived near Pinewood hated it -they never expected to have a volcano on their doorstep. Then the plasterers and riggers demanded danger money because they were working so high up. But, as often happened on the Bond films, the team got so excited about doing something that had never been done before that they ended up working day and night, and at the weekend they'd bring their families along to look at it. I suppose now you'd use CGI but we tried not to cheat the audience. When we showed 500 stuntmen sliding on ropes down from the roof there really were 500 men."

(629) Tomorrow Never Dies was called 007 and the Empire of Tomorrow in Romania.

(630) Although most Bond fans would probably agree that Never Say Never Again could have been a lot better, it got incredible reviews when it first came out. The Chicago sun Times likened the return of Connery to a Beatles reunion.

(631) The acclaimed American director Katherine Bigelow said she was badgered by Sony Pictures chief Amy Pascal to direct a James Bond film but declined these offers. Bigelow, had she been interested, would have become both the first American and the first woman to direct a Bond film.

(632) The Goldeneye script had to be rewritten to eliminate similarities to the 1994 James Cameron spy action film True Lies.

(633) The Fort Knox set at Pinewood for Goldfinger had to have 24 hour security in case thieves tried to steal the gold bar

props.

(634) When he was cast as James Bond, Timothy Dalton read all the Ian Fleming novels in preparation for the role.

(635) The early Goldeneye script by Michael France was set in post-Soviet Russia and revolved around Augustus Trevelyan - a former Double O agent who was a mentor to Bond. Trevelyan betrayed MI6 and defected to the Soviet Union during the Cold War. His actions caused the death of two British agents so Bond is sent on a personal revenge mission. Trevelyan seeks to control an EMP satellite weapon and Bond naturally has to foil these plans. While you can clearly detect the bare bones of what would become Goldeneye in France's script there are a number of differences between this early draft and what we actually got on the big screen in 1995. Trevelyan is a much older character in France's script than the more youthful Trevelyan portrayed by Sean Bean in the movie.

(636) Brigitte Bardot was the first choice to play Tracy in On Her Majesty's Secret Service but she preferred to make a movie called Shalako with Sean Connery instead.

(637) Timothy Dalton originally turned down the part of Bond in 1986 because he was appearing in a play and also signed up for a Brooke Shields film called Brenda Starr. After losing Pierce Brosnan because of Remington Steele's return, Dalton became available again because his play had ended. Cubby Broccoli offered to push production on The Living Daylights back six weeks so Dalton could do Brenda Starr first and then become Bond. However, Dalton was still reluctant to take the role. After mulling the offer over for a while, Dalton finally agreed to become James Bond while he was sitting in an airport hotel in the United States waiting for a flight.

(638) The early plan for Licence To Kill was to shoot the film in China and two story treatments (which included a motorbike chase along the Great Wall) were written with this in mind.

Unfortunately though the success of the film The Last Emperor nixed this plan and made the idea of going to China feel far less novel or fresh.

(639) Roger Moore said in his memoir that he did not get along with Grace Jones very well on A View To A Kill because their dressing rooms were quite close and she would constantly play loud rock music.

(640) When he was told that he had been chosen to become James Bond, Roger Moore said he celebrated by having oysters and martinis with the director Guy Hamilton.

(641) The actual shooting script for No Time To Die was only completed weeks before the film began shooting. Because of all the shenanigans with Danny Boyle and John Hodge leaving the project, there hadn't been a huge amount of time to knock the new screenplay into shape.

(642) Sela Ward was considered for the part of Paris Carver in Tomorrow Never Dies.

(643) Max Von Sydow played Blofeld in Never Say Never Again but most of his scenes ended up on the cutting room floor - to the point where it seemed pointless to have hired him the first place!

(644) Cubby Broccoli used to be partners with the famous American producer Irwin Allen. When Cubby told Allen he wanted to option the Bond books, Allen told him the Fleming novels were awful and wouldn't even be worthy of television.

(645) Richard Brownjohn, Maurice Binder's assistant, did the title sequence for Goldfinger. These titles are a slight departure but very stylish and iconic. Scenes from the film are projected onto gold painted women.

(646) Cubby Broccoli said that he wanted to cast Julie Christie

as Domino in Thunderball but Terence Young thought her chest was too flat to be a Bond girl.

(647) Anthony Hopkins was heavily courted to play Eliot Carver in Tomorrow Never Dies but he declined the part because the script wasn't ready.

(648) Goldfinger was so popular that some cinemas ran 24 hour a day screenings in order to meet demand.

(649) Irvin Kershner had only seen two Bond films when he directed Never Say Never Again. He had no great interest in James Bond and only did the film as a favour to Sean Connery.

(650) Ace of Bass were in contention to do the Goldeneye theme. The demo for their rejected theme was later turned into a song called The Juvenile.

(651) The For Your Eyes Only poster featured Bond in the background seen through the (long and shapely) legs of a model. The original version of this poster earned protests from Christian groups because the model was showing too much buttock (if you'll pardon the expression). In the end a pair of denim shorts was added to the model in the poster to make it less risque.

(652) At 106 minutes, Quantum of Solace is the shortest Bond film.

(653) Bond producer Michael G. Wilson played an extra in Goldfinger and then became a tax lawyer. After co-producer Harry Saltzman left the franchise in the early 1970s, Cubby brought Michael G Wilson (who was his step-son) back into the 007 business and Wilson has been there ever since. Wilson had also established a tradition of making a Stan Lee style cameo in every Bond film.

(654) George Lazenby only discovered that George Baker had dubbed some of his OHMSS dialogue (where 007 poses as

genealogist Sir Hilary Bray) when he watched the film. Lazenby was not best pleased by this.

(655) On Her Majesty's Secret Service grossed $82 million from a $7 million budget.

(656) The first drafts of the Goldeneye script were written for Timothy Dalton.

(657) In preparation for designing his Fort Knox set in Goldfinger, Ken Adam was allowed to tour the Fort Knox site but he was not actually allowed inside the building.

(658) The script for Licence To Kill borrowed a few elements from the Fleming short story The Hildebrand Rarity. The Hildebrand Rarity appeared in the 1960 short story collection For Your Eyes Only.

(659) Jessica Biel was considered for the part of Strawberry Fields in Quantum of Solace.

(660) One could argue that the film version of Goldfinger makes one ingenious change from the novel which actually makes it work better than the book. In the film they had the clever idea of Goldfinger seeking to set off a dirty bomb in Fort Knox - thus flooding the gold with radiation and therefore greatly increasing the value of his own gold reserves.

(661) The end of Diamonds Are Forever was originally supposed to feature frogmen leaping out of helicopters and attaching mines to Blofeld's oil rig.

(662) Cameraman and professional skier Willy Bogner, Jr. was the man responsible for the amazing ski sequences in On Her Majesty's Secret Service, The Spy Who Loved Me, and For Your Eyes Only. Bogner was especially good at capturing footage while skiing backwards!

(663) Timothy Dalton is very popular with Bond fans but

never got a chance to consolidate his Bond with casual audiences. A third film would have gone a long way to achieving this.

(664) In the 007 auditions for Goldeneye, Sean Bean impressed the producers enough to secure the consolation prize of rogue Double O villain Alec Trevelyan in the movie.

(665) George Lazenby went to a voice trainer before he auditioned for Bond in an attempt to tone down his Australian accent.

(666) In what was considered to be a surprising decision, the American actor John Gavin was originally signed by Broccoli & Saltzman to play Bond in Diamonds Are Forever. Gavin was best known for playing Sam Loomis in Psycho and a Bondish spy in O.S.S 17 Double Agent. Gavin was certainly handsome but a bit wooden. United Artists were not enthused at all by Gavin and decided to go all out to get Sean Connery back. This required the studio to pay a then unheard of fee amounting to $1.25 million (which Connery donated to charity), support two film projects of Connery's choice, and also pay the actor compensation for any overrun in the weekly shooting schedule. The unlucky John Gavin was compensated financially by the studio for the termination of his contract and drifted into television roles. In 1981 he became the United States Ambassador to Mexico.

(667) When Brosnan left the role of Bond, Colin Salmon (who played Charles Robinson in the Brosnan films) made no secret of his desire to become the new 007. This obviously didn't come to pass. It would have felt rather weird for Bond fans if Charles Robinson had suddenly become James Bond in the next movie!

(668) Sean Connery said that one of the things which soured him on the Bond films was that he felt they became increasingly silly and obsessed with hardware and gadgets. "They started getting into all this space stuff. They kept upping

the physical hardware. I mean, that car going through the alley on its side in Diamonds Are Forever — it just got to be too much."

(669) Barbara Carrera designed her own costumes as Fatima in Never Say Never Again because she couldn't find any clothes outrageous enough for her character in traditional fashion houses.

(670) William Gaunt tested to play James Bond in Live and Let Die. Gaunt was best known for playing Richard Barrett in the fantasy action TV show the Champions.

(671) Telly Savalas was scared of flying and had a 'no flying' clause written into his contract when he signed to play Blofeld in On Her Majesty's Secret Service.

(672) A View To A Kill is essentially a remake of Goldfinger with Silicon Valley replacing Fort Knox.

(673) The character of Paloma in No Time To Die was largely crafted by Phoebe Waller-Bridge and a fairly late addition to the script.

(674) There were a lot of stories in the media in 1988 that Cubby Broccoli had offered the part of the villain in Licence To Kill to the musician Gene Simmons of Kiss but this obviously didn't transpire in the end.

(675) When it comes to Champagne, Fleming and Bond prefer Taittinger to Bollinger.

(676) Roger Moore said his favourite Bond gadget was 007's magnetic watch in Live and Let Die.

(677) David Prowse (aka Darth Vadar and the Green Cross Code Man) was considered for the part of Jaws.

(678) Moonraker grossed a whopping $210.3 million. This was

a relief for Cubby Broccoli because it cost $34 million to make.
Adjusted for inflation, Moonraker had a budget of over $120
million in today's money.

(679) The late New Zealand actor David Warbeck claimed that
he was something akin to a substitute Bond during the Cubby
era. Warbeck, who was a sort of a cult B-movie action and
horror star because of the many films he made in Italy, almost
became James Bond in the early 1980s when the director John
Hough was hired to develop a Bond film. Hough had made a
film called Wolfshead (aka Wolfshead: The Legend of Robin
Hood) with Warbeck and Cubby Broccoli decided that David
Warbeck would be a sensible choice as the new 007 because he
knew John Hough. In the end though, Roger Moore, as ever,
decided to come back and dashed Warbeck's Bond dream.

(680) Catherine Deneuve was considered for the part of
Solitare in Live and Let Die.

(681) The American model Talisa Soto, who had only a few
acting credits at the time, was chosen for the part of Lupe in
Licence To Kill after Davi said she was the most beautiful of
the women they had tested.

(682) Production on Octopussy was briefly halted when Roger
Moore appeared to have heart problems. It turned out to be a
false alarm though and he was given a clean bill of health.

(683) Ken Adam's amazing hollowed out volcano sets for You
Only Live Twice had a sliding roof and working monorail.

(684) Cubby Broccoli said he was the only one who could deal
with Sean Connery because Connery hated Harry Saltzman
and would barely speak to him.

(685) James Mason was someone the producers seriously
considered for the part of Bond in Dr No.

(686) Before production began on Live and Let Die, Tom

Mankiewicz had lunch with Sean Connery in a charm offensive that EON hoped might persuade Connery to do the film. It was of course unsuccessful. "I always hear that it's my ******* obligation to play James Bond," Connery told Mankiewicz. "I've done six, when does my ******* obligation stop? After ten, twelve, fifteen?"

(687) Lorraine Chandler recorded a theme song for You Only Live Twice that wasn't used.

(688) Actresses who appeared in both Bond films and Hammer Horror films include Jenny Hanley, Shirley Eaton, Madeline Smith, Caroline Munro, and Valerie Leon.

(689) Burt Reynolds said he was approached a couple of times to play James Bond in the early 1970s but ruled himself out because he felt Bond should be played a British actor. Reynolds later said he regretted this decision and should have gone for the part.

(690) Radiohead submitted a song for the Spectre theme but it was rejected in favour of Sam Smith.

(691) John Woo turned down an offer to direct Goldeneye.

(692) No Time To Die went through four scripts before it started shooting.

(693) Terence Stamp said he was considered as a replacement for Sean Connery in the late 1960s but scuppered his chances because his unusual take on what approach to take. "I was taken out to dinner by Harry Saltzman and he put it out there that he'd be interested in me doing it. I was flattered, but felt so self-conscious because Sean had been so successful, so identified with it. I said to Harry: 'Let's do the one where Bond is disguised as a Japanese. I'd play the whole film in the disguised make-up and at the very end, you see it's me!' I thought this very unusual idea would get over the self-consciousness of there suddenly being a different 007.

Needless to say, I never heard from him again!"

(694) Sam Mendes has admitted that 2015's Spectre had its third act rewritten during shooting.

(695) Sylvia Trench was supposed to return in Goldfinger but Guy Hamilton axed this plan when he took over as director from Terence Young.

(696) A View To A Kill was called Murder In The Eyes in Israel.

(697) Roger Moore said that when he became James Bond he presumed that he'd make a couple of films and then the franchise would have run its course. In the end he made seven Bond movies.

(698) The studio thought the name Pussy Galore in Goldfinger was too risque and mulled over changing the character's name to Kitty Galore.

(699) Goldeneye spawned one of the most famous video games of all time with 1997's classic first person shooter Goldeneye 007. This was a wonderful turn of events for EON because it made James Bond a much more visible brand to young people.

(700) George Lazenby said that, in hindsight, he had been very stupid by walking away from Bond after one movie. Lazenby noted that Connery was shrewd in that he only quit Bond after he had made plenty of money from it. Lazenby was foolish enough to quit Bond before it made him rich!

(701) Cubby Broccoli and Harry Saltzman (perhaps because they didn't get on well in the end) seemed to almost alternate their producing duties on the Bond films. If, for example, you read Roger Moore's Live and Let Die Diaries (which is an entertaining behind the scenes account of making his debut Bond film) you will notice that Moore mentions Harry Saltzman a lot more than he does Broccoli. Saltzman was

obviously the more hands on producer when they made Live and Let Die.

(702) Before Bond 15 became The Living Daylights, Michael G. Wilson drafted a treatment which was essentially an origin story. Wilson's script treatment had a twentysomething Bond teaming up with a veteran agent to battle a Chinese warlord named Kwang. By the end of the story, the veteran agent is dead and Bond has inherited his mantle and become a full fledged secret agent. The story would show us how Bond met M, Q and Moneypenny for the first time.

(703) The French Navy supplied the frigate and Eurocopter Tiger you see in Goldeneye.

(704) Tomorrow Never Dies had its entire script jettisoned as it entered production.

(705) In 1990, Alfonse M. Ruggiero Jr and Michael G Wilson wrote a Bond 17 story treatment for a third Timothy Dalton film but - sadly - this film never came to pass because of litigation between EOn and the studio over television rights. The litigation dragged on until the end of 1992. It would be 1995 before Bond was back on the big screen and Dalton was gone by then.

(706) The Bond 17 script treatment by Alfonse M. Ruggiero Jr and Michael G Wilson concerned the handover of Hong Kong from Britain to China (which was set to happen in 1997). An accident at a British chemical weapons plant leads to Bond investigating Sir Henry Lee Ching - a British-Chinese entrepreneur. The story takes place in Hong Kong, Japan, and China, and has Bond teaming up with a female master thief and part-time CIA agent named Connie Webb. Now that the Cold War was apparently no more, the Bond team obviously looked to China (as the remaining communist superpower at the time after the fall of the Soviet union) for inspiration when it came to intrigue and villains.

(707) Persis Khambatta, best known for Star Trek: The Motion Picture fame, was in contention for the title role in Octopussy but lost out to Maud Adams.

(708) The bungee jump which begins Goldeneye was shot in Locarno, Switzerland.

(709) Barbara Carrera said she turned down a part in Octopussy so she could be in Never Say Never Again with Sean Connery.

(710) It is sometimes reported that The Living Daylights was originally written for Roger Moore but this was not the case.

(711) George Lazenby and director Peter Hunt fell out during the production of On Her Majesty's Secret Service. Lazenby said that they barely spoke to each other for much of the shoot.

(712) The Spy Who Loved Me grossed $185.4 million from a $14 million budget.

(713) In his memoir, John Glen said that he fell out with Timothy Dalton near the end of production of Licence To Kill and they had a shouting match while shooting the final scene.

(714) In early plans for the 2015 Bond film Spectre, M was going to revealed to be a villain and traitor. However, this idea was abandoned when the actor Ralph Fiennes voiced his displeasure and said he didn't want to play M as a villain.

(715) In 1992, the newspapers were full of unlikely stories that the Hollywood producer Joel Silver was planning to buy the James Bond franchise and replace Timothy Dalton with Mel Gibson. In the midst of the litigation wrangles (which prevented production on a third Dalton film going ahead) it was reported that Cubby Broccoli put his Bond rights up for sale and Silver was one of the interested parties. However, this sale obviously did not go ahead. Broccoli either never planned to sell in the first place, withdrew his offer, or was simply

using the threat of a sale as a tactic in his battle with former MGM/UA owner Kirk Kerkorian and MGM's Giancarlo Parretti - an Italian financier who purchased MGM for $1.2 billion in 1990.

(716) Bond fans thought it was a bit of a swizz that Bond's Z3 Roadster in Goldeneye is never seen in action. This was because the car was a late addition to the film and only a prototype that the producers were not allowed to damage.

(717) Adolfo Celi's voice in Thunderball was dubbed by Robert Rietty (who previously dubbed the voice of John Strangways in Dr No). Rietty later dubbed the man who appears to be Blofeld in the For Your Eyes Only PTS.

(718) Talisa Soto later said that Lupe in Licence To Kill was much tougher and more morally dubious in the original script and that the character was changed and softened somewhat. "Lupe was truly a villain at first, but as we were working there were rewrites. They decided to soften her up and make her fall in love with James Bond."

(719) Michael Billington, a square jawed and hairy chested actor best known for Gerry Anderson's UFO and The Onedin Line, was used by EON to play 007 in screen tests for prospective Bond actresses in the seventies and early eighties. Billington was very nearly cast as Bond in Live and Let Die but lost out to Roger Moore. He was then given a part in the PTS of The Spy Who Loved Me as Sergei Barsov, the lover of Soviet agent Anya Amasova. Billington was more or less an employee of EON and ready to step into 007's shoes at any moment should there be a problem with Roger Moore. Roger and Cubby would usually have some wrangles over Roger's salary for each new film before Roger (usually at the last minute) signed on the dotted line so Cubby liked to have a plan B up his sleeve. Michael Billington was plan B for much of Roger's era.

When they were preparing For Your Eyes Only, Roger Moore's

participation was not set in stone so Michael Billington was flown to Corfu (one of the locations for the film) and given a full costume test. In the end though, Roger Moore did the picture and Billington wasn't needed. Billington said that the same thing happened with Octopussy a few years later. Once again, Roger Moore decided to come back and Billington wasn't needed.

(720) Danny Boyle was the original director of Bond 25 (or No Time To Die as it became). Danny Boyle's time on Bond 25 lasted about six months in total. Boyle's departure from Bond 25 was due to what is commonly known in the film industry as creative differences.

(721) In the end, Cary Joji Fukunaga was announced as the new director of Bond 25 a month after Danny Boyle left the project. The fact that Fukunaga was the first American to direct a Bond film was strange but more of an accident than a set rule. There was never any stipulation that American directors couldn't direct a Bond film and that Bond directors must be British or from commonwealth countries (as Martin Campbell, Roger Spotiswoode, and Lee Tamahori had been). In the early 1990s, the American director John Landis (of Blues Brothers, Trading Places, Animal House, and An American Werewolf in London fame) had been under consideration to direct Timothy Dalton's doomed third Bond adventure until litigation mothballed the franchise for several years.

(722) Bond fans used to wonder if Finlay Light was even real. A newspaper article in 1986 claimed he was a 32 year-old Australian model who had signed a ten year contract to become the new Bond but any evidence of Finlay Light being a real person was thin on the ground. However, while he didn't get the part he was actually real. John Glen confirmed in his memoir that Finlay Light tested for The Living Daylights.

(723) Cary Fukunaga said that he had championed Billie Eilish for the No Time To Die theme song and had to persuade the

producers it was a good idea. They didn't seem to know who Billie Eilish was. You could probably forgive Michael G. Wilson and Barbara Broccoli if they weren't totally up to speed on the latest teenage music sensation.

(724) Tiffani Thiessen auditioned for the role of Dr Christmas Jones in The World Is Not Enough.

(725) Sadly, a stunt man was killed shooting the bobsleigh ski chase in For Your Eyes Only.

(726) 80`s punk band Blondie recorded a For Your Eyes Only theme song. However, when Blondie were asked to record the song again to improve it they declined to do so and Sheena Easton was hired instead.

(727) Die Another Day grossed $435 million from a $145 million budget.

(728) From Russia with Love made $79 million from a $2 million budget.

(729) The title song for Licence To Kill was originally supposed to be done by Eric Clapton. There was apparently a plan to eschew a traditional title song and have a reworked version of the Bond theme over the titles.

(730) Barbara Bach was a friend of United Artists Executive Danton Rissner. Rissner asked Cubby Broccoli if he could find her a small part in The Spy Who loved Me and she ended up as the female lead.

(731) After he'd left the role of Bond, Pierce Brosnan said - "When I played Bond, it'd been dormant for six years; it was a huge undertaking on the part of everyone involved to get it right. And so I was kind of caught somewhere in between the Roger Moore and the Sean Connery of it all. And both men, I adored as James Bond. But it never felt—I don't know—real. I felt like I was in a period-piece sometimes."

(732) The 1987 film The Living Daylights was called His Name Is Danger in Chile.

(733) The New York Times didn't like The Man with the Golden Gun much when it was released - 'The throbbing information that "the energy crisis is still with us" isn't what you need or want to learn from a James Bond picture. But that poverty of invention and excitement characterizes Guy Hamilton's "The Man With the Golden Gun," which opened yesterday at neighborhood theaters. The movie, which also explains that "coal and oil will soon be depleted," sets Bond in pursuit of a missing device that converts solar energy into electricity Bored already? That was predictable, Even Kingsley Amis, a great admirer of the late Ian Fleming, spoke of "the over-all inferiority" of the writer's last novel, and this movie is doggishly faithful to its model. There's a male villain with three nipples, but you can't milk much plot out of that—or them.

Amid the general lack of gumption, Roger Moore's large rigid figure appears to be wheeled about on tiny casters I always have a soft spot for statues that turn out to be alive, and there are a couple in this film.But an actor who appears to have been cast in clay is another matter, and Mr. Moore functions like a vast garden ornament. Pedantic, sluggish on the uptake, incapable of even swaggering, he's also clumsy at innuendo. (While Sean Connery wasn't the wit of the century, he did manage to be impudent, and there were those pleasing moments of self-parody.)

But whether Mr. Moore is twisting a woman's arm to discover a fact that he already knows, or nuzzling an abdomen without enthusiasm, he merely makes you miss his predecessor. The script trundles out such lines as "Your steam bath is ready" or "A mistress cannot serve two masters" between the dullest car chase of the decade and a very routine explosion. The only energetic moments are provided by Herve Villechaize, as a midget gifted with mocking authority, and Christopher Lee as the golden gunman—both have a sinister vitality that cuts through the narrative dough. (Yet if I were a midget, I'd rebel against the perky bass music that bubbles up at every entrance; cute bassoons did the same for the dwarf in "The Abdication." Can't small persons be filmed without coy theme tunes?) The movie also includes some beautiful glimpses of Thailand. But if you enjoyed the early Bond films as much as I did, you'd better skip this one.'

(734) The late Michael Winner (best known for directing the first three Death Wish movies with Charles Bronson) claimed in his memoir that he turned down the chance to direct Live and Let Die. Winner said he later regreted this decision. "I don't know why I turned down James Bond. I can't imagine. I took the call right there, 1971. 'Are you interested in James Bond?' they said. 'Harry Saltzman would like you to do it.' I said, 'No.' I mean, it's not as if I was making Hamlet! Oh, no thanks, I only do Ibsen! I was only doing thrillers anyway. A moment of lunacy."

(735) Terence Young once said - "If you asked me what were the three ingredients for James Bond, it was Sean Connery, Sean Connery and Sean Connery!"

(736) A Die Another Day spin-off film featuring Halle Berry as Jinx almost went ahead until MGM pulled the plug.

(737) Sam Mendes wanted Sean Connery to play Kincaid in Skyfall but they didn't bother to approach Connery because they knew he'd say no. Albert Finney played the part in the end.

(738) It always feels kind of insulting when Bond leading ladies today imply their character will be strong and independent and quite unlike Bond Girls of the past. Have they never heard of Diana Rigg or Honour Blackman?

(739) Renny Harlin was approached about directing Goldeneye in its very early stages but he said he wasn't

interested because they were still planning on using Timothy Dalton at the time. Harlin obviously didn't think that Timothy Dalton was a very good Bond.

(740) Pierce Brosnan has admitted that he didn't get on very well with Teri Hatcher when they made Tomorrow Never Dies. Brosnan had lobbied for Monica Bellucci to play Paris Carver.

(741) George Lazenby breaks the fourth wall at the end of the PTS of On Her Majesty's Secret Service by saying - "This never happened to the other fella!" This was a line Lazenby said on the set all the time so the director Peter Hunt decided to have him say it in the film.

(742) In the Las Vegas car stunt in Diamonds Are Forever there is a continuity blooper when the Mustang comes out of the alleyway the wrong way up compared to how it went in.

(743) Every fresh script rewrite on Never Say Never Again had to be approved by an insurance company lest it should flout Kevin McClory's strictly defined Bond rights (which permitted to remake Thunderball - NOT make up his own Bond film) and give Cubby Broccoli any fresh legal ammunition.

(744) Chiwetel Ejiofor was the first choice to play c in Spectre but Andrew Scott played this part in the end. Leaked SONY emails suggested that they hired Scott because he was cheaper.

(745) The legendary Bond composer John Barry had a cameo in The Living Daylights as an orchestra conductor.

(746) Peter Anthony was a young model who won a Daily Express competition to find the perfect James Bond for Dr No. He actually got an audition on the back of the publicity.

(747) Priscilla Presley was considered for the part of Stacey Sutton in A View To A Kill.

(748) Marcus Gilbert was another actor considered for the part

of James Bond in The Living Daylights. Gilbert was a dashing actor with male model good looks who had appeared in The Masks of Death (starring Peter Cushing as Sherlock Holmes) and Biggles: Adventures in Time. Gilbert would become best known for the television miniseries Riders.

(749) In Kevin McClory's aborted 1977 Bond film Warhead, Shrublands is not a health farm but a scuba-diving school for agents.

(750) A View To A Kill was called From A Lethal Viewpoint in Sweden.

(751) It takes seventeen minutes for James Bond to make an appearance in the movie From Russia with Love.

(752) Pierce Brosnan had a beard and long hair at the press conference unveiling him as James Bond because he was about to shoot a Robinson Crusoe film.

(753) The Living Daylights was called Scared to Death in Hungary.

(754) Faye Dunaway was up for the part of Domino in Thunderball but then had a change of heart and ruled herself out.

(755) The helicopter PTS of For Your Eyes Only was suggested by director John Glen. Cubby Broccoli didn't care much for the idea because he didn't think it was exciting enough to open a Bond film. However, they couldn't think of anything else so Cubby eventually gave the go ahead to Glen to shoot the helicopter sequence. Use of miniature model helicopters was combined with real helicopter footage in the sequence.

(756) During production on The Spy Who Loved Me in Egypt, the crew were said to be in low spirits because of the heat and poor quality of the food. Cubby Broccoli had pasta and tomatoes flown in, took over a local restaurant, and personally

cooked spaghetti bolognaise for the entire cast and crew. This raised morale and made Cubby even more popular.

(757) In one of his last interviews, Desmond Llewelyn said of George Lazenby - "I know about George from what he has told me later. He wasn't an actor, he was a car salesman. It was jolly bad luck with him really. When he met Cubby and he asked him to do a test, he had never met an actor and didn't know what a test was. He spent a couple of days looking for actors, to find out what happened. Then some idiot said you're a star now behave like one. He had only read in the papers how stars behaved off the set, such as getting drunk and having a good time. What he didn't realise was on the set they were highly professional people, they didn't argue with the director, they learnt their lines, they were on time. Lazenby just behaved extremely badly."

(758) If you include audiobooks, short films, and video games, over two hundred people have played James Bond.

(759) James Bond uses more gadgets in Moonraker than any other movie.

(760) Will Sampson was considered for the part of Jaws. Sampson was best known for his part as Chief Bromden in One Flew Over the Cuckoo's Nest.

(761) Licence To Kill grossed $156.1 million from a $32 million budget

(762) Guy Hamilton was somewhat disparaging about the latest Bond films in a 2003 interview. "Now we see nothing but explosions and bang-bangs, and the stunts are not really very interesting with the trick photography; the FX man is always on top of it. When we did stunts, the stuntman jumped out of a six-floor window into a wet sponge, and if he missed the sponge, he could seriously hurt himself. But at least you knew he jumped. Sean Connery and Gert Froebe played scenes, that's what I don't see in the latest Bond films. You've

got to set a problem for Bond, you've got to talk about something."

(763) Christopher Lee, the villain in The Man with the Golden Gun, was the cousin of Ian Fleming.

(764) In a 2012 interview, Barbara Broccoli reflected on realism and violence in Bond films and seemed to suggest that, in her view, Licence To Kill might have gone a little too far. "When we did Licence to Kill, that was a lot more violent," she reflected. "It was the first one that got a 15-rating in the UK, and I think we overstepped the mark there, in terms of going a bit too far into the realism. So that's something we're always struggling with. When to be realistic, and if so, how realistic and how much."

(765) Saffron Burrows was considered for the part of Miranda Frost in Die Another Day.

(766) Ian Fleming supposedly has a small cameo in from Russia with Love during a train scene.

(767) Right up until the week that Never Say Never Again was due to hit cinemas, Cubby Broccoli and EON were still in court trying to block the film's release.

(768) In his career after James Bond, it is claimed that Sean Connery was very forensic when it came to profit share deals on movies and even hired accountants for the specific task of investigating the profits of each film he made to make sure he wasn't being short-changed. This was no doubt a reaction to his sense that Broccoli and Saltzman had short-changed him on the Bond films.

(769) Sean Connery didn't turn up to Cubby Broccoli's memorial service in 1996. Roger Moore, Timothy Dalton, and Pierce Brosnan posed together at this event.

(770) Jane Fonda is alleged to have been offered the role of

Tiffany Case in Diamonds Are Forever. She had no interest in the part though.

(771) Bo Derek was considered for the role of Stacey Sutton in A View To A Kill.

(772) Billie Eilish and her brother Finneas said that their James Bond theme took only three days to write. They said they listened to past Bond themes in preparation for crafting the song.

(773) Kristina Wayborn as Magda broke some toes shooting a scene in Octopussy when he character has to kick a weapon out of a goon's hand. The bazooka she had to kick was supposed to be plastic but turned out to be metal.

(774) For Your Eyes Only grossed $195.3 million from a $28 million budget.

(775) Kate Bush was approached to sing the theme song for Moonraker but declined because she was about to go on tour and simply didn't have the time.

(776) The motorbike stunt (when the bike jumps over the chopper) in Tomorrow Never Dies was done in one take by stunt rider Jean Pierre Goy. He had to clear a forty-four foot drop at 60 mph. The rotor blades of the helicopter were added in with CGI afterwards.

(777) Daniela Bianchi was dubbed by Barbara Jefford in From Russia with Love.

(778) Sean Connery did not have to audition when he became James Bond. He insisted that he wouldn't do a screen test.

(779) Honor Blackman was the oldest Bond girl until Monica Belluci in Spectre. Blackman was 37 when she made Goldfinger.

(780) When The Living Daylights was released, a sniffy Derek Malcom in The Guardian wrote - "You no longer expect more than you get, and by now are left noting only the fine tuning of the formula. Dalton hasn't the natural authority of Connery nor the facile charm of Moore, but George Lazenby he is not. It's an able first go in the circumstances, though perhaps it could do with a bit more humour."

(781) The Daniel Craig era has what you can only describe as an awkward chronology in that Craig's Bond seemed to go from rookie agent to world weary veteran in the space of about one film. The Craig era seems curiously light on Bond just being an agent undertaking missions. It feels like a chunk of his 'career' is missing.

(782) Goldfinger was briefly banned in Israel when it was reported in the media that Gert Frobe was a former member of the Nazi Party. Frobe left the Nazi Party in 1937. It transpired that Frobe had actually helped hide and rescue Jews during the war.

(783) Rupert Friend was interviewed for the part of Bond in Casino Royale. Friend was deemed to be a strong candidate but decided to rule himself out of contention. Friend later starred in the television show Homeland.

(784) In Fleming's Dr No book, it is a deadly centipede rather than a tarantula that is placed in Bond's bed.

(785) Harold Sakata, who played Oddjob in Goldfinger, won a silver medal for the United States in Light-Heavyweight wrestling in the 1948 London Olympics.

(786) In 1992, it was reported in the media that a James Bond television show was in the works and that Robert Powell and Lewis Collins were among the actors who had been approached to play James Bond in this proposed show. To the surprise of absolutely no one, these stories turned out to have no basis in fact. Even so, EON took the step of publishing a

statement (more of a warning really) in Variety reminding any 'interested parties' that only they had the legal rights to make films or television shows based on James Bond.

(787) Sharon Stone had discussions about the part of Pam Bouvier in Licence To Kill. At the time, Stone wasn't very well known.

(788) The former world boxing champion Glenn McCrory said he read for the part of James Bond in 1994. He's not the only boxer who has been linked to Bond. The boxer turned actor Gary Stretch was widely reported to have done an audition for Casino Royale in 2005.

(789) Believe it or not, Pierce Brosnan's Aston Martin V-12 Vanquish in Die Another Day is based on real technology. If you give something a mirrored surface it can be made to appear invisible.

(790) On February the 2nd, 2020, a 30-second spot for No Time to Die ran late in the second quarter of the Super Bowl. Commercials for the Super Bowl cost more than $5 million each for 30 seconds.

(791) The actor Simon Oates said he was all but cast as James Bond in Diamonds Are Forever and his agent was negotiating a fee. However, at the last minute Sean Connery decided to come back and Oates had his Bond hopes dashed.

(792) There were plans for David Hedison to return as Felix Leiter in The Man with the Golden Gun but they couldn't find a way to write Leiter into the story.

(793) Milton Reid, who played Sandor (the fellow Bond holds up by his tie before dropping him from the buiding) in The Spy Who Loved Me, was previously in contention to play Oddjob in Goldfinger. Reid was also in the first Bond movie as one of Dr No's guards.

(794) The decision to 'reactivate' Remington Steele had had equally frustrating consequences for Pierce Brosnan's co-star Stephanie Zimbalist, who played Laura Holt in Remington Steele. Zimbalist had been cast as Officer Lewis in Paul Verhoeven's Robocop but had to abandon the film and go back to making Steele with Brosnan. She was replaced in Robocop by Nancy Allen.

(795) When the Daniel Craig era began back in 2006 there was a sense that Bond had fallen behind the times because of the Jason Bourne films. The Bourne Identity, a 2002 Doug Liman thriller based on a book by Robert Ludlam, was about an amnesiac spy (played by Matt Damon) who travels through Europe trying to unravel his identity as a number of assassins and the CIA follow his trail. The Bourne Identity showed that you didn't need hundreds of millions of dollars to make a great action thriller. It had fantastic car chases, brutal fight sequences, and a compelling story. The Bourne Identity had a kinetic energy at times that the recent Bond films seemed to lack. 2004's sequel The Bourne Supremacy was also a critical and box-office success. The shaky camera style of new director Paul Greengrass was not universally loved by everyone but there was no question that The Bourne Supremacy was a rollicking ride and a terrific action film. The Bourne films were tough, mean, and lean and Bond, the producers decided, had to follow suit if the franchise was to stay relevant.

(796) Claudine Auger, who played Dominique "Domino" Derval in Thunderball, was a former Miss France.

(797) Roger Moore said in his memoir that Maurice Binder used to drive Cubby Broccoli mad because he'd only complete his Bond title sequences at the last minute as the premiere loomed.

(798) The Man With The Golden Gun made $161.8 million from a $7 million budget.

(799) David Bowie turned down the part of villain Max Zorin

in A View To A Kill. "I didn't want to spend five months watching my double fall off mountains," said Bowie.

(800) Rami Malek's condition for accepting the part of Safin in No Time To Die was that the villain should have no political or religious ideology. No one was planning to do this anyway so EON were happy to accept this condition.

(801) It is estimated that James Bond has been shot at over 4000 times in the movie franchise.

(802) In 1956, Bob Holness provided the voice for James Bond in a South African radio adaptation of the Ian Fleming novel Moonraker. Holness would later become familiar on British television for hosting quiz shows.

(803) Barbara Broccoli was the producer on the big tanker chase in Licence To Kill. You might say that Barbara finished her apprenticeship on the Timothy Dalton films.

(804) Tomorrow Never Dies was supposed to begin with a mountain climbing PTS but this plan was obviously abandoned in the end. Roger Spottiswoode said the sequence was abandoned because it would have been too dangerous to shoot.

(805) Bond ordering the tiger to "sit!" in Octopussy is a reference to Barbara Woodhouse. Barbara Woodhouse was a dog trainer who often appeared on British television in the 1980s.

(806) After a few initial outbursts at NBC, Pierce Brosnan showed his class by mostly staying silent about losing out on The Living Daylights. He did this largely out of respect for Timothy Dalton - who he personally knew and also liked. Brosnan did though shoot a 007 inspired Diet Coke commercial in 1988 in which he played a James Bondish Milk Tray Man style character who dodges ninjas and hangs on the side of the train before settling down in a carriage to enjoy a

can of coke with a beautiful woman.

(807) An Aston Martin used in Goldfinger sold at a 2010 auction for $4.6 million.

(808) Anita Ekberg and Julie Christie were under consideration for the role of Honey Ryder in Dr No.

(809) Richard Todd was one of Ian Fleming's preferred choices to play James Bond in Dr No. Todd was a British actor best known for films like The Dam Busters and The Longest Day. He was a war hero in real life too. It is believed that Todd had existing commitments to other films when they were casting for Dr No and so could not be considered in the end.

(810) David Hedison injured both his knees shooting the parachute scene where Bond and Leiter land back at the church in time for Leiter's wedding to Della in Licence To Kill.

(811) Believe it or not, Roger Moore had a firearms phobia.

(812) A-Ha's lead singer Morten Harket was offered a small role as a villain's henchman in The Living Daylights but he declined this invitation.

(813) Dan Romer was supposed to compose the score for No Time To Die but he was replaced by Hans Zimmer. Romer's departure was due to that old chestnut 'creative differences'.

(814) Strawberry Fields covered in oil in Quantum of Solace is obviously a homage to Shirley Eaton in Goldfinger.

(815) Timothy Dalton said that it was extremely rough shooting some of the explosive tanker chase scenes (not to mention the climax where sets light to Felix - triggering a massive explosion) in Licence To Kill and that it rather put him off doing stunts in the future.

(816) Daniel Craig's trainer Simon Waterson said that Craig

spent a year getting into shape for No Time To Die. His routine involved punishing workouts and a strict diet. A typical breakfast for Daniel Craig at this time was rye bread, poached eggs, avocado and kimchi, kale, and turmeric, lemon, and ginger shots. Craig would eat vegetarian meals for most of the week and abstain from alcohol.

(817) Before he directed the 80s Bonds, John Glen worked as an editor and second unit director. Perhaps his finest hour in this capacity was the pre title sequence of The Spy Who Loved Me where Bond skis off a mountain range into infinity before his Union Jack parachute opens. It was Glen who hiked up a mountain in Baffin Island with his film unit to capture this legendary stunt.

(818) The Living Daylights grossed $191.2 million from a $40 million budget.

(819) Christopher Lee was one of the names floated for the part of Dr No in the first Bond movie. Lee said he was never approached though.

(820) Goldfinger is generally considered to be the film that established the Bond formula or blueprint. Cubby Broccoli felt however that From Russia with Love was the movie which set in stone the Bond template.

(821) In a set visit to the production of Licence To Kill, Garth Pearce noted that Timothy Dalton hadn't let becoming James Bond change him at all as a person. Dalton still lived in the same modest house he'd had since before he became Bond and still did all his own shopping.

(822) Robert Wagner claims that Cubby Broccoli was interested in him playing Bond. Wagner told Broccoli that an American couldn't play Bond and suggested Cubby hire his friend Roger Moore instead.

(823) George Lazenby was actually forwarded part of his

salary for Diamonds Are Forever. He had to return the money.

(824) Roger Moore said he was horrified when he saw the sequence in A View To A Mill where Max Zorin guns down the mine workers. Roger thought it was too violent for a Bond film.

(825) Ian Fleming visited the set of Goldfinger a couple of times but, sadly, he died before the film was released.

(826) Richard Maibaum said that after Jack Lord, they deliberately made the Felix Leiter actors look dumpy or ordinary so as to make James Bond look better.

(827) There was some criticism when it came to light that Rami Malek's villain in No Time To Die would have a scarred face in the film. Some felt this 'villain trope' (the idea that having a facial disfigurement or scar makes someone appear sinister or evil) was rather insensitive in this day and age. It should be noted though that Bond himself has a facial scar in the Ian Fleming books.

(828) Although the Bond franchise has been deemed rather sexist in its treatment of women at times it has also been surprisingly progressive. Women in Bond films have been astronauts, pilots, spies, assassins, and even the head of MI6!

(829) The villain Dr No was based on Sax Rohmer's Fu Manchu.

(830) The Disco Volante, Largo's yacht in Thunderball, was built at a cost of over $100,000 by production designer Ken Adam.

(831) The keel-hauling sequence from Fleming's Live and Let Die novel was supposed to take place in the 1973 movie of the same name. In the end it appeared in For Your Eyes Only.

(832) Believe it or not, there was actually a lot of scepticism

regarding 1995's Goldeneye before it was released. When the cast was unveiled, the British press noted the absence of big stars and even suspected that this film was maybe being made on the cheap or something.

(833) Clint Eastwood was approached about playing James Bond after Sean Connery left but he had no interest in the part. Eastwood felt that James Bond should be played by a British actor and that it wasn't really his type of thing anyway.

(834) The threat of legal action by Kevin McClory had prevented EON from using Blofeld for decades. A character who seemed an awful lot like Blofeld was used for a joke in the pre-title sequence of For Your Eyes Only but, this aside, Blofeld had been absent from the official Bond films since we last saw him in Diamonds Are Forever. This meant that Roger Moore, Timothy Dalton, and Pierce Brosnan never tangled with Blofeld in any of their films.

(835) Julian Glover was considered for the part of Bond in the early seventies. A decade later he played the villain in For Your Eyes Only.

(836) Sean Connery never liked James Bond's Aston Martin DB5. Connery called it a "ladies car" and felt it was too small and uncomfortable.

(837) Never Say Never Again grossed $160 million from a $36 million budget.

(838) Harry Saltzman intended Thunderball to be the first Bond film but the McClory legal case with Fleming obviously complicated that and made them change their plans.

(839) Cubby Broccoli said they considered Oliver Reed playing Bond when Sean Connery left for the first time. "Oliver Reed was very near the top of the list. Lazenby was an unknown. We could mould Lazenby into the public perception of James Bond, into the kind of Bond we knew the fans wanted. With

Oliver Reed we would have had a far greater problem. Oliver already had a public image; he was well known and working hard at making himself even better known. We would have had to destroy that image and rebuild Oliver Reed as James Bond – and we just didn't have the time or the money."

(840) United Artists threatened to pull the plug on Dr No when the film overran its production budget. It's a good job they didn't. The entire course of cinematic history might have been altered!

(841) The late Amy Winehouse was the producers' choice for the Quantum of Solace theme song but her well documented personal problems meant her song was never completed.

(842) Prince Charles visited the No Time To Die set at Pinewood Studios on the 20th of June 2019 and met with the cast and crew. Prince Charles took a great interest in the cars on the Bond 25 set and was shown the Aston Martin by Daniel Craig. 10 DB5s were used in Bond 25. Prince Charles joked to reporters that he had been offered a cameo in the film and was now considering whether or not to accept the offer. You will not be surprised to learn though that Prince Charles decided in the end not to launch an acting career and accept a Michael G Wilson or Stan Lee style cameo in Bond 25.

(843) On Her Majesty's Secret Service was originally supposed to follow Thunderball in the film series. At one point, Sean Connery was actually under contract to appear in On Her Majesty's Secret Service. In the end they obviously decided to do You Only Live Twice next.

(844) From Russia with Love is the Bond movie that establishes gadgets as a big part of the franchise.

(845) Despite the remarkable longevity of the Bond series there are a surprising amount of Fleming titles and scenes yet to make it into the film franchise. Risico and The Property of a Lady are among the yet as unused Fleming titles.

(846) Diamonds Are Forever grossed $120 million from a $7.5 million budget.

(847) Sean Connery, famously, was a milkman when he was a young man.

(848) Die Another Day was called Morre Noutro Dia in Portugal. The translation is A New Way To Die.

(849) In 1959, Ian Fleming wrote an article about what he would do if he was made Prime Minister for a day. Fleming wrote - 'I should proceed to a complete reform of our sex and gambling laws and endeavour to cleanse the country of the hypocrisy with which we so unattractively clothe our vices. To deal only with my most far-reaching proposal, I would consult with my Minister of Leisure about the possibility of turning the Isle of Wight into one vast pleasuredome which would be a mixture of Monte Carlo, Las Vegas, pre-war Paris and Macao. Here there would be casinos (they are building one on Gibraltar and they have one in Nassau; why not one on the Isle of Wight?) and the most luxurious maisons de tolérance in the world. Bingo, poker, faro, fan-tan, craps— even whist drives with money prizes!'

(850) The Aston Martin crash in Casino Royale broke a world record for the most amount of car flips in a stunt.

(851) Peter Morgan's rejected script treatment (for what became Skyfall) was titled Once Upon a Spy and would have featured flashbacks featuring Judi Dench's M as an MI6 operative during the Cold War. 'Once Upon a Spy would have flashed back to M's days as an MI6 agent stationed in Berlin during the cold war,' wrote the Guardian. 'Her affair with a KGB agent has lasting ramifications three decades later when the man's son, a Russian oligarch, surfaces to blackmail the spymaster. Bond is called in to tackle the villain, but is forced to kill M at the movie's denouement. "[Co-writer] Neal [Purvis] and I are pretty well steeped in Fleming. I think Peter

was more interested in Le Carré. It just didn't work," said writer Robert Wade, according to Digital Spy. "We always found [the script] really, really difficult to make credible or satisfying. It was very dark. The only thing that remained was that M's past comes back to haunt her and she dies at the end."'

(852) Heineken reportedly paid $45 million to get their beer in Skyfall.

(853) Downtown Las Vegas was closed for five nights so that the car chase in Diamonds Are Forever could be shot.

(854) The recasting of the lead actor naturally gives the Bond franchise a temporary injection of freshness and novelty. Goldeneye and Casino Royale were both evidence of this. The Living Daylights (whatever anyone might try to retrospectively tell you about the Timothy Dalton era) was also very well received in 1987. A Bond film that marks the debut of a new lead actor is always hugely anticipated.

(855) Fleming's literary Bond has a preference for Russian or Polish vodka.

(856) Bond does not appear in the PTS for Live and Let Die nor The Man with the Golden Gun (unless you count a waxwork dummy). Strictly speaking, Bond doesn't appear in the From Russia with Love PTS.

(857) No Time To Die was fairly unique in the way that it was marketed as Daniel Craig's last film. It was hard to think of this ever happening in the Bond franchise before. A View To a Kill, for example, has no sense of being the last Roger Moore film. At the time they didn't know if it was definitely Roger's last film but at 57 years of age they must have suspected that it probably would be. Even so, there is no pause for reflection or any nostalgia in A View To a Kill. It's simply another Bond film with Roger Moore.

Die Another Day gives no hint that this is Pierce Brosnan's last film because at the time it was obviously assumed that Brosnan would be back. Licence To Kill has not the barest hint of being Timothy Dalton's last film because at the time they had no idea the series was about to go into mothballs and were already making vague plans for the third Dalton adventure. Even when Sean Connery made his one-shot return to play Bond in Diamonds Are Forever there wasn't any attempt to market or reference the fact that this was Connery's last go around. The reason for this was presumably that United Artists still hadn't given up on the idea of him coming back again.

(858) An actor named Mark Greenstreet auditioned to play Bond for The Living Daylights. Greenstreet later said that during a break he went to use the toilet and bumped into Michael Biehn in his Corporal Hicks colonial space marine costume (James Cameron was shooting Aliens at the studio while Greenstreet's auditions took place).

(859) EON haven't cast a really young actor as Bond since George Lazenby. Even Daniel Craig (who was supposed to be a young Bond new to the service in Casino Royale) was a rather mature looking 38 year-old when he got the part.

(860) In early plans for the 2015 film Spectre, Blofeld was going to be a woman or an African warlord. These ideas were obviously abandoned.

(861) Roger Moore said he had no reservations whatsoever about taking over as James Bond. He said it was like playing Hamlet (in that there were others before him and would be others after him).

(862) Casino Royale was the first Bond film to be shown in mainland Chinese cinemas.

(863) A New Zealand actor called Roger Green tested to play Bond in Diamonds Are Forever. Green played rugby for the

junior All Blacks. "The director sat me down and said 'Roger, you've got a great chance of getting this part'," said Green. "I drank for a week on that one. Ten people did the test that day and one by one were told they were not wanted, except for me. Then I read in the paper a couple of months later 'Sean Connery agrees to do two more Bonds'."

(864) Matthew Vaughn (the director of Kingsmen: The Secret Service) claimed that he was supposed to direct Casino Royale until Martin Campbell came along but EON have never commented on this. "I had a lot of meetings on Casino Royale," said Vaughn. "So much so that the head of MGM offered me it. I had a 24-hour period where I thought I was directing Casino Royale."

(865) Paul Dehn, a writer on the early Bond films, definitely deserves more credit and acclaim for the role he played in establishing the formula of the movie franchise. Dehn, who was also a poet, left the Bond franchise early. He said that "all that kiss kiss bang bang stuff" wasn't for him. He later did a lot of writing for the Planet of the Apes movie franchise.

(866) Two time Bond Girl Maud Adams is a background extra in A View To A Kill. She visited the San Francisco set to hello to Roger Moore and so they put her in a crowd scene.

(867) Shirley Anne Field turned down the part of Jill Masterson in Goldfinger.

(868) Susie Coelho was considered for the title role in Octopussy. Coelho is an English born actress and businesswoman of Indian heritage.

(869) Drax's henchman Chan in Moonraker is played by Toshiro Suga. Suga was Michael G. Wilson's akido instructor.

(870) No Time to Die was the first time the Daniel Craig era had fallen back on the old Bond trope of using 'die' or 'kill' in the title.

(871) The producer Jack Schwartzman had to dip into his own pocket to get Never Say Never Again finished when the film ran over its budget.

(872) Of his Bond novels, Ian Fleming wrote - 'My plots are fantastic, while being often based upon truth. They go wildly beyond the probable but not, I think, beyond the possible. . . . Even so, they would stick in the gullet of the reader and make him throw the book angrily aside—for a reader particularly hates feeling he is being hoaxed—but for two further technical devices, if you like to call them that.

First of all, the aforesaid speed of the narrative, which hustles the reader quickly beyond each danger point of mockery and, secondly, the constant use of familiar household names and objects which reassure him that he and the writer have still got their feet on the ground. This is where the real names of things come in useful. A Ronson lighter, a 4.5 litre Bentley with an Amherst-Villiers supercharger (please note the solid exactitude), the Ritz Hotel in London, the 21 Club in New York, the exact names of flora and fauna, even James Bond's Sea Island cotton shirts with short sleeves. All these details are points de repère to comfort and reassure the reader on his journey into fantastic adventure.'

(873) The Spy Who Loved Me cost twice as much as any previous Bond film.

(874) Because it was not known if Roger Moore was coming back, For Your Eyes Only was written in a rather generic way when it came to James Bond in the film. The opening scene where Bond places flowers on his wife's grave was written to connect a new Bond actor to the history of the franchise.

(875) Pierce Brosnan was supposed to do a fifth film but Barbara Broccoli and Michael G. Wilson decided to reboot the franchise with a new actor (who obviously turned out to be Daniel Craig). On being removed as James Bond, Pierce

Brosnan later said - "I did my full contract, which was for four movies; they invited me back, and I remember distinctly being in the beach house in Malibu and the phone rang, and Michael and Barbara [Cubby's heirs] said, "We'd love you to do the fifth." And I said, "I'd love to." I put the phone down; I said to my wife, Keeley, I said, "OK. Go build your dream-house. Because I'm doing a movie. They've just invited me back." And then I went off to do a movie in that interim time, After the Sunset, and one day I was going out onto the set, and the phone rang, and it was my agent, and they said, "Listen. They've started negotiations on the film." I said, "OK, what does that mean?" He says, "Well, they don't want to negotiate anymore. They'll call you next Thursday." I said, "OK." So I waited a whole week, and then the next Thursday came, and I was in the Bahamas—I think I was staying at Richard Harris's house with Richard and his family; there's an interconnectedness there. And Michael and Barbara said they'd rethought the character and were putting it on hold and we said goodbye.

And that was it. Alright. You were a good Bond. So that's how it went down that time. And that certainly dug into the solar plexus of life, just because it was pretty gut-wrenching and because it had been somewhat heralded that I was coming back. So, it's just business. And you're the one caught in the crosshairs. And, you know, my press agent at the time said, "You should resign. You should resign." And I said, "No, I don't want to do that, because that's a lie. It's a lie onto myself; it's their decision. Let it be their decision, and however you want to look at it, however it will be defined, then let it find its own course." So you get on and you work. You just get back in the ring, and try to define yourself and not let there be angst over it. Head up, shoulders back. So yeah, there's those kind of blows"

(876) In Kevin McClory's aborted 1977 Bond film Warhead, the story had Blofeld stealing nuclear weapons in order to blackmail the United Nations into handing over control of the world's oceans to SPECTRE.

(877) Desmond Llewelyn said that Terence Young wanted him to play Q as a Welshman. This idea was scrapped though. "What he wanted was me to play it as a Welshman," said Llewelyn. "I had a helluva fight with him because I told him it wouldn't work as I could only do a broad Welsh accent, and a south Welsh accent. He wouldn't have been a Major with that type of accent. In the end I said is this what you want: (breaks into a strong Welsh accent) "... and This lovely case I got here, I just press a button and out comes a knife!" He said no, no, so I played him as a toffee nosed Englishman ever since."

(878) In 2013, Live and Let Die star Madeline Smith said - "I will be hated for this reply. I prefer the 'old' Bonds: Connery, Moore and Brosnan, and think all the 'ladies' came out of it quite well. The more recent harsher, tougher women appear to reflect today's society, which I don't care for."

(879) Live and Let Die made $161.8 million from a $7 million budget.

(880) In 2012, Christopher Wood (who helped write the scripts for The Spy Who Loved Me and Moonraker), said of the current Bond films - "I am not shaken and stirred by 'new' Bond. The movies seem like imitations of the Bourne series and I find Daniel Craig, though a good actor, akin to a muscle-bound Hobbit. I miss the lightness of touch of the old Bonds and having shifted uneasily through Casino Royale was not tempted to see the next one."

(881) Billie Eilish is the youngest artist to write and perform a Bond theme.

(882) When he was interviewed on the set of The Spy Who Loved Me for the BBC, Roger Moore admitted that he didn't have the faintest idea what the plot of the film was!

(883) The New York Times gave Moonraker a glowing review in 1979 when the film was released. 'At a time when everything

is being either inflated or devalued it's comforting to know
that at least one commodity maintains its hard currency.
That's James Bond, who, by all rights, should be an antique, as
emblematic of the 60's as the Beatles and flowerpower, but
who goes blithely on as if time has had a stop."Moonraker,"
which opens today at the Rivoli and other theaters, is the 11th
in the remarkable series that began in 1963 with "Dr. No" and
it's one of the most buoyant Bond films of all. It looks as if it
cost an unconscionable amount of money to make, though it
has nothing on its mind except dizzying entertainment, which
is not something to dismiss quickly in such a dreary,
disappointing movie season. Almost everyone connected with
the movie is in top form, even Mr. Moore who has a tendency
to facetiousness when left to his own devices. Here he's as
ageless, resourceful and graceful as the character he inhabits.'

(884) Ian Fleming's short story The Living Daylights revolves
around Bond's distaste for killing - despite it often being an
unavoidable part of his job. This story would be incorporated
into the beginning of the 1987 Timothy Dalton film of the
same name in faithful fashion.

(885) Sean Connery was said to have found it amusing that
Ian Fleming - the ultimate establishment figure - lost his court
case in an English court to an Irish outsider like Kevin
McClory. This is probably one of the reasons why Connery
liked McClory. Not only was mcClory a means for Connery to
get back at Cubby Broccoli, Connery also admired McClory's
plucky underdog status in the movie world.

(886) Roger Moore said he got banged up quite badly shooting
the ice hockey sequence in For Your Eyes Only.

(887) The late Yaphet Kotto, who played the villain Live and
Let die, was rather disparaging about the film in a 2012
interview. "There were so many problems with that script... I
was too afraid of coming off like Mantan Moreland. I had to
dig deep in my soul and brain and come up with a level of
reality that would offset the sea of stereotype crap that Tom

Mankiewicz wrote that had nothing to do with the Black experience or culture. It was the first Black Bond villain, I wanted to be original but there was nothing I could draw on from Tom's script. It was a trap. If I had played it the way it was written, every Black Organization in the world would have been on my case. I had to draw on a real life situation I was going through and that saved me. But the way Kananga dies was a joke... and... well... the entire experience was not as rewarding as I wanted it to be. There were a lot of pitfalls that I had to avoid, and I did."

(888) When Diana Rigg passed away in 2020, George Lazenby wrote on social media - 'I'm so sad to hear of the death of Diana Rigg. She undoubtedly raised my acting game when we made On Her Majesty's Secret Service together in 1968-9. I remember the press conference at the Dorchester in London, knowing she was going to play my wife. We had fun together on the set of the movie in Switzerland and Portugal. Her depth of experience really helped me. We were good friends on set. Much was made of our supposed differences but that was the Press looking for a news story. I was sorry to have lost my wife in the film at the end. The death of Contessa Teresa di Vincenzo Draco created a memorable cinema moment over 50 years ago. As my new bride, Tracy Bond, I wept for her loss. Now, upon hearing of Dame Diana's death, I weep again. My deepest condolences for her family.'

(889) Batman star Adam West claimed that Cubby Broccoli offered him the part of Bond when Sean Connery left.

(890) Ken Adam's amazing volcano set in You Only Live Twice used 700 tonnes of structural steel.

(891) Tomorrow Never Dies made $355 million from a $125 million budget.

(892) Broccoli and Saltzman do not have a producing credit on Thunderball - despite the fact that they obviously co-produced the film. They were clearly trying to placate Kevin McClory by

giving him the credit. They must have suspected that McClory could be a potential thorn in the side of EON (and they were not wrong about that).

(893) Sean Connery was born as Thomas Connery on 25th August 1930 in Edinburgh.

(894) Desmond Llewelyn does not appear as Q in Live and Let Die. This was a consequence of the producers wanting to downplay gadgets. Llewelyn was rather irritated by this because he had already arranged some time off from the TV show Follyfoot in anticipation of appearing in Live and Let Die. He was also a friend of Roger Moore so had even more reason to want to be in the film.

(896) Thunderball won an Academy Award for best special effects.

(897) John Barry was asked to score Goldeneye but he was too busy and wanted to spend time with his family. It has been alleged that Barry turned them down because they weren't willing to offer him enough money. It's a great shame because Goldeneye would have been enhanced even further by a John Barry score. There are videos on YouTube where John Barry cues have been put over the Goldeneye tank chase and the immediate difference it makes is incredible.

(898) Robert Bathurst, later best known for the television show Cold Feet, claims he tested to play Bond for The Living Daylights but thought it was only to put pressure on Timothy Dalton to make a decision. Bathurst was about 30 at the time and had mostly appeared in comedy shows. "Oh, that was such a ludicrous audition," said Bathurst. "I could never have done it - Bond actors are always very different to me. But some casting director persuaded me to go. The thing was, they already had Timothy Dalton. But I think he hadn't signed yet so they wanted to tell him, 'They're still seeing people, you know,' to put pressure on him to sign. I was just an arm-twisting exercise."

(899) Around 75% of the women James Bond has taken to bed have tried to kill him in the end.

(900) Maud Adams made history when she took the title role in Octopussy as she had already played a Bond Girl in The Man with the Golden Gun.

(901) From Russia with Love is alleged to be the last film John F. Kennedy watched before he was assassinated.

(902) A View To A Kill grossed $152.4 million from a $30 million budget.

(903) James Bond's family motto is 'Orbis Non sufficit' - which translates to 'The World is not enough'.

(904) Up until the novel Dr No, Bond used a Beretta M418. However, when Ian Fleming received a letter telling him that the Beretta M418 was a 'ladies gun', he gave Bond a Walther PPK.

(905) The Service Armourer in the Bond books is named Boothroyd after the man who wrote to Fleming complaining that the Beretta was a rubbish gun for Bond.

(906) Daniel Craig is the 'booziest' Bond in that his version of the character is seen drinking alcohol more often than the others.

(907) The director John Glen was quite keen on Highlander star Christophe Lambert playing Bond in The Living Daylights but Lambert's heavily accented and not exactly fluent English made this an unlikely prospect.

(908) Roger Moore said he didn't like the scene in For Your Eyes Only when Bond kick Loque's car off the cliff. He felt it was a bit too ruthless for his lighter take on Bond.

(909) Goldfinger grossed $125 million from a $3 million budget.

(910) Although the relationship between Cubby Broccoli and Harry Saltzman was difficult when their Bond partnership ended, several years later Cubby invited Harry to the premiere of For Your Eyes Only to show there were no hard feelings.

(911) The Australian actor Andrew Clarke (who looked a lot like Tom Selleck and even had a tache) was another Australian candidate to play James Bond in The Living Daylights. In his memoir, John Glen said that Clarke was a 'front runner' for quite some time. Clarke played Simon Templar in a 1987 TV film pilot.

(912) Daniel Craig was the first actor under six foot in height to play James Bond.

(913) When they were discussing who should become the first ever James Bond actor in Dr No, Cubby Broccoli said that Ian Fleming mentioned Roger Moore but that he (Broccoli) felt that Roger looked too young and foppish at the time. Roger Moore later said that no one ever approached him about Dr No.

(914) Karl Urban said he spoke to Barbara Broccoli about playing James Bond in Casino Royale but he was so busy he was never able to do an audition. It appears though that she had her heart set on Daniel Craig anyway.

(915) George Lazenby claimed that after he quit the Bond franchise, Cubby Broccoli used his influence to have Lazenby shunned in the film industry. It's obviously impossible to verify these allegations.

(916) Michelle Yeoh was invited to return as Chinese super agent Wai Lin in Die Another Day but she was too busy to accept the offer.

(917) 'No villain matches Sanchez for menace,' wrote Den of Geek in a retrospective article about Licence To Kill. 'If he uncovered Bond, he would kill Bond. Simple as that. Not quite 'why don't you just shoot him' because Sanchez wouldn't just shoot him. He'd exact a far nastier retribution. But exact it he would. No locking Bond in a windowed room, no escorting Bond round the pad and feeding him dinner, no leaving Bond in a perilous situation and then departing for tea. If Sanchez wanted Bond dead, Bond would be killed. Thoroughly. Such ruthlessness is refreshing and admirable on the writers' behalf. Franz Sanchez is unquestionably the great forgotten villain of the franchise. He possesses all the vital characteristics: charm, intelligence, ruthlessness.'

(918) In 1995, when Goldeneye was released, Timothy Dalton said he saw a big billboard of Pierce Brosnan as 007 and felt a sense of relief. Dalton was grateful for the fact that it was Brosnan and not him who now had to do all the interviews, chat shows, and photo shoots to promote the film.

(919) Gary Russell in Starburst gave The Living Daylights a fantastic review when it came out in 1987. "If not the best Bond, then certainly up there with From Russia With Love, Eyes Only and On Her Majesty's Secret Service... The most impressive factor in the film, the one on which its success depends more than the story, is one Timothy Dalton, who is so damn good as James Bond you feel like asking where he's been since Connery left. Although he's only done this one [and there's still no confirmation he's signed for another] I feel safe to proclaim Dalton the best of the four, and one that Ian Fleming would have approved of... All in all, The Living Daylights has paved the way for a further twenty-five years of good James Bond films, and that is largely due to Timothy Dalton, who deserves as much credit as possible."

(920) In Kevin McClory's aborted 1977 Bond film Warhead, the temporary headquarters of SPECTRE was going to be inside the Statue of Liberty.

(921) When Moonraker was released in 1979, Gene Siskel in the Chicago Tribune took issue with the movie's gratuitous product placement. 'In the beginning of the Bond series, before they were thought of as a series, each film was a good action picture with a colourful, entertaining hero. Today, they come off as conglomerate business enterprises rather than movies. How else does one explain the intrusive commercial plugs in Moonraker for Christian Dior perfume, British Airways, Bollinger champagne, Glaston boats, and Seiko watches? Truly, money derived from these plugs can't be worth the loss of story continuity when the products are flashed in front of the camera. Someone is being awfully cheap about the plugs, which borders on incredibility because the James Bond series is one of the surest moneymakers in the film business. Maybe the producers of Moonraker are blind to story construction?'

(922) Ian Fleming was known to contradict himself from time to time in the Bond books. You can probably forgive these occasional memory lapses. In one book he said Bond hated beef and yet in another book he said that Bond lived on beef.

(923) Roger Moore said that he liked as much action as possible in his Bond films because this meant he had fewer lines to learn!

(924) The reaction to Daniel Craig's casting in 2005 was underwhelming. Most people had never heard of him. Craig gave a poor impression at his first press conference by chewing gum and not displaying much in the way of personality. The Sun called him James Bland. You could say Daniel Craig had the last laugh in the end.

(925) Multiple scripts were commissioned for The Spy Who Loved Me. In one of the drafts, the villain had a secret base at Loch Ness.

(926) Thunderball stuntman Bill Cumming was given a $450 bonus to plunge into Largo's shark infested pool.

(927) One of Barbara Broccoli's jobs on A View To A Kill was to make sure that Grace Jones got to the set on time. This was no easy task because Grace Jones hated early mornings. It is believed that Barbara's diplomatic skills were considerably enhanced by the experience of sharing a car with a grumpy Grace Jones at the crack of dawn!

(928) The original concept for The Spy Who Loved Me's PTS was completely different and had Bond on a raft before surfing ashore.

(929) Roger Moore was friends with Cubby Broccoli and Harry Saltzman several years before he became Bond. Harry Saltzman was actually his neighbour for a while.

(930) Peter Burton played Major Boothroyd (Bond's gadget supplier) in Dr No. Burton chose not to return for the next films because he was busy doing other things. It was a decision he later regretted. Desmond Llewelyn became Q thereafter.

(931) The director Martin Campbell wanted to cast Henry Cavill as Bond in Casino Royale. This may explain why Campbell seemed a trifle grumpy in the press conference that unveiled Daniel Craig.

(932) "I couldn't see myself taking over and not doing it my own way," said Timothy Dalton of Bond, "to try and capture Fleming's Bond. He's tarnished. He's not a superclean hero. He's not a white knight. He drinks, smokes. He suffers from this thing called accidie, a moral malaise or confusion which makes him... thoroughly like us."

(933) Fleming's Bond will sometimes add a tot of whiskey to his coffee.

(934) The title of You Only Live Twice is taken from a 300-year-old poem by the Japanese poet Basho.

(935) Sean Connery is the only Bond actor who had to wear a toupee for most of his films.

(936) Sam Neil auditioned to be Bond in The Living Daylights. He said that he was pressured into the audition by a bossy agent and that it was the worst day of his life.

(937) Timothy Dalton insisted that Bond should not sleep with Lupe early in Licence To Kill (as had been planned) because Lupe had been exploited by men and it would seem as if Bond was just using her in the same way.

(938) The elephant hunt in Octopussy was originally supposed to take place in The Man with the Golden Gun.

(939) On average, the cinematic Bond has a drink every 10 minutes, 53 seconds.

(940) Guy Hamilton said it was surprisingly difficult to persuade Roger Moore to get his hair cut when he became James Bond. Hamilton insisted that James Bond should always have short hair.

(941) Albert Finney had discussions about playing Carver in Tomorrow Never Dies but nothing came of this in the end. Finney would later appear in Skyfall.

(942) The Man with the Golden Gun's 'bendy bridge' car stunt was the first stunt to be calculated on a computer before it went ahead.

(943) The ski scene in For Your Eyes Only was shot in Cortina d'Ampezzo, Italy, in the Alps. The producers had a big problem though because there was hardly any snow there at the time. They had to import ice, snow, and powder to lend an appropriately ice-glazed backdrop.

(944) John Cleese took over as Q in the Bond films for Die Another Day after playing 'R' in The World Is Not Enough.

However, Cleese was not retained and Pierce Brosnan left the role - something which all seemed to irritate Cleese. "I did two James Bond movies," he said, "and then I believe that they decided that the tone they needed was that of the Bourne action movies, which are very gritty and humorless. Also the big money was coming from Asia, from the Philippines, Vietnam, Indonesia, where the audiences go to watch the action sequences, and that's why in my opinion the action sequences go on for too long, and it's a fundamental flaw. The audiences in Asia are not going for the subtle British humor or the class jokes."

(945) Sean Connery said he barely got any sleep on the first week of shooting Diamonds Are Forever. He spent all night shooting the film and then played golf during the day.

(946) Rick Sylvester, who performed the ski jump in the PTS of The Spy Who Loved me, said that when he went to a preview screening he heard a member of the audience say to the person next to them that it must have been a dummy or mannequin that went off the mountain because no one could possibly have done that stunt in real life!

(947) The role of Max Zorin was offered to Sting after David Bowie turned it down but he passed too. It didn't turn out too badly though because they got Christopher Walken in the end.

(948) Adolf Hitler shot himself with a Walther PPK.

(949) Madeline Smith said she felt somewhat uncomfortable shooting the scenes in Live and Let Die when her character Miss Caruso is cosying up to Bond because Roger Moore's wife was on the set that day watching them do the scene.

(950) The door code to the bio-room in Moonraker is the theme from Close Encounters of the Third Kind. Steven Spielberg had to be asked permission to use this. In return, Spielberg was allowed to use the James Bond theme in The Goonies several years later.

(951) A Rolex watch worn by Bond in On Her Majesty's Secret Service sold at an auction in 2013 for $41,000.

(952) One very shrewd thing the Bond franchise did after Timothy Dalton era was move the release dates of the films to the winter rather than the summer. This has generally meant that Bond films will now open at a time when there is less competition at the box-office. It isn't always this simple (Tomorrow Never Dies famously found itself up against James Cameron's Titanic - but then who would have guessed that Titanic would be so insanely popular and make two billion dollars?) but, for the most part, opening Bond films around October or November has been a profitable strategy and new tradition for EON.

(953) The Disco Volante is Italian for flying saucer.

(954) Roger Moore's Bond kissed more women than any of the other cinematic Bonds. Roger's Bond kissed a total of 24 women in his movies.

(955) Dolph Lundgren made his first screen appearance in A View To A Kill as one of Zorin's goons. He has no lines in the film. Lundgren was dating Grace Jones at the time - which might explain why he got his part in the film.

(956) You Only Live Twice is rather unique because it's the only film where Bond is not seen driving.

(957) Ursula Andress was overdubbed by Nikki Van der Zyl in Dr No.

(958) Titos Vandis tested for the part of Auric Goldfinger. You can find his screen test on YouTube.

(959) The crime author Donald Westlake was one of the first writers to have a stab at writing Bond 18 (or Tomorrow Never Dies as it became). 'The first storyline to be properly

considered came from crime novelist (and Oscar-nominated screenwriter) Donald Westlake,' wrote Fiction Machine. 'He had been commissioned to develop a treatment and returned with a story about the United Kingdom's handover of Hong Kong back to the People's Republic of China. 'Westlake's treatment, which came with suggested titles such as Dragon's Teeth, Never Look Back and On Borrowed Time, pitched Bond against the rich American businessman Gideon Goodbread. Goodbread – described by Westlake as 'John Goodman with a Southern accent' – had a plan to rob Hong Kong's banks before sinking the entire city.

Barbara Broccoli and Michael Wilson were not happy enough with Westlake's treatment, particularly the Hong Kong setting; it was clear that Bond 18 would not be completed until late 1997, at which point the Handover would be several months out of date. Of Westlake's pitch, the only elements that continued through to the finished film were the idea of pitting Bond against a wealthy businessman, and pairing Bond with a female Chinese agent while defeating him. Donald Westlake returned to his original storyline in 1998, adapting it into the original novel Forever and a Death. It was ultimately published by Hard Case Crime in 2017, nine years after Westlake's death.'

(960) The original plan for On Her Majesty's Secret Service was to end with Bond's wedding and then have Tracy killed in the PTS of the next movie. The director Peter Hunt dug his heels in though and insisted that OHMSS should have a downbeat ending.

(961) While he was James Bond, Pierce Brosnan was prohibited from wearing a tuxedo in any other movie.

(962) The girls portrayed as the pilots in Pussy Galore's Flying Circus were actually men dressed up.

(963) Roger Moore was the first Bond to have a digital watch.

(964) In a deleted scene cut from The Living Daylights, Q branch demonstrate a pen that can mimic any handwriting. Just the thing to forge a document!

(965) The PTS of Tomorrow Never Dies and the Hamburg scenes with Bond and Q had already been shot before the script was completely revamped. Brosnan shot these scenes while he was on a promotional tour for the movie Dante's Peak.

(966) Sheena Easton shot her contribution to the title sequence of For Your Eyes Only in just a single day.

(967) There's a curious contradiction with Sean Connery's attitude to Bond in that he always expressed his displeasure with the escalating hardware and gadgets and yet when he was a story consultant on Kevin McClory's Warhead the resulting story treatment was very fantastical and hardware heavy with robotic sharks and all manner of outlandish mayhem.

(968) Ben Whishaw said that the director Cary Fukunaga worked in an improvisational way on No Time To Die and was always willing to change something if he didn't feel a scene was working to his satisfaction.

(969) Jill St John was originally cast as Plenty O'Toole in Diamonds Are Forever but then upgraded to the significantly larger role of Tiffany Case.

(970) SMERSH is the consolidated version of the Russian phrase smert shpionam, meaning death to spies.

(971) There was never any confirmation about who would have played Bond in Kevin mcClory's Warhead film but it seems unlikely that Sean Connery wouldn't have been tempted in the end. It's hard to think of any alternative (and plausible) option in 1977 who would have had the stature of Connery.

(972) Barbara Bach was given the part of Anya Amasova in

The Spy Who Loved Me only days before the film began shooting. Bach wasn't the greatest actress in the world and director Lewis Gilbert had to do multiple takes for some of her scenes.

(973) Lois Maxwell was originally offered the part of Sylvia Trench in Dr No but she preferred the part of Moneypenny.

(974) Aside from Mission Impossible, the other big action franchises in the Daniel Craig era have been the Fast and the Furious and Marvel movies. The connected nature of the Marvel movies has some parallels with the Daniel Craig era. It would be inaccurate though to say that they had an influence on the Bond series when it came to long form storyteling because the Marvel films only really kicked into gear with 2008's Iron Man - by which time the Daniel Craig era was already two films old and committed to a continuity (of sorts) rather than the usual stand alone adventures. Serialised storytelling is something that seems to be in vogue. The TV shows we binge require us to pay attention and remember what has gone before. Blockbuster film franchises like Twilight and Harry Potter used serialised storytelling.

(975) Hans Zimmer said that there was a 'box' of potential Bond themes they had to listen to for No Time To Die before they picked one and these included a Billie Eilish demo. Zimmer felt that was definitely the right one to choose - although he claimed that EON weren't so convinced at first. Zimmer had never met Billie Eilish before and suggested they fly her over to London to work on the theme. Eilish arrived in Soho suffering from jet lag and was shown some of No Time To Die so that she knew what sort of mood the film was going through.

(976) Gerry Anderson threatened legal action when The Spy Who Loved Me came out because he claimed it bore similarities to the Moonraker treatment he had written for Harry Saltzman several years previously. He was persuaded to drop his case in the end. The Moonraker script treatment that

Gerry Anderson and Tony Barwick wrote for Harry Saltzman in the early 1970s had a villain named Zodiac and identical triplet henchmen. Zodiac was hijacking nuclear submarines in the story so you can see why Anderson threatened legal action when 1977's the Spy who loved Me came out.

(977) The imposing Julie T Wallace, who plays Rosika Miklos (Bond's Bratislava contact at the TransSiberian Pipeline) in The Living Daylights, came to the attention of the Bond producers with her fine breakthrough performance on British television the previous year as Ruth in the cult miniseries The Life and Loves of a She-Devil.

(978) Daniela Bianchi was Miss Universe in 1960.

(979) A first edition of the Casino Royale novel can go for over £5,000.

(980) Thunderball was the first Bond film shot in widescreen.

(981) George Lazenby said he found Diana Rigg a bit snooty on the set of On Her Majesty's Secret Service. Lazenby said that Rigg seemed to think she was the star of the film. If rumours are to believed though, they had a brief affair making this movie.

(982) Carey Lowell said she didn't know that much about Bond films when she got the part of Pam Bouvier in Licence To Kill so for her research she simply started renting James Bond movies from the video store to watch!

(983) The actress playing 007's leading lady has only been older than the actor playing James Bond twice. Honour Blackman was three years older than Sean Connery when they made Goldfinger and Diana Rigg was a year older than George Lazenby when they featured in On Her Majesty's Secret Service. Monica Belluci was older than Daniel Craig in Spectre but she wasn't really playing the leading lady.

(984) In May 1976, Kevin McClory took out an advert in
Variety in which he said that production on Warhead would
begin in Febuary 1977. This obviously didn't happen in the
end.

(985) Goldie Hawn was considered for the part of Solitaire in
Live and Let Die.

(986) Octopussy grossed $183.7 million from a $27.5 million
budget.

(987) The katana-wielding goon Bond battles in Osato's office
in You Only Live Twice is played by Peter Fanene Maivia -
grandfather of Dwayne Johnson.

(988) Out of the Bond films he made, Roger Moore said The
Spy Who Loved Me was his favourite.

(989) Christopher Nolan is always linked to the director's
chair on each new Bond film but (at the time of writing) this
has yet to happen. "I've spoken to the producers Barbara
Broccoli and Michael G Wilson over the years," Nolan said in
2017. "I deeply love the character, and I'm always excited to
see what they do with it. Maybe one day that would work out.
You'd have to be needed, if you know what I mean. It has to
need reinvention, it has to need you. And they're getting along
very well without me." Bond fans couldn't help noticing
Nolan's OHMSS riffs in Inception and the great love for The
Spy Who Loved Me that Nolan often expresses in interviews.
Christopher Nolan said that a childhood experience of
watching The Spy Who Loved Me inflamed his passion for the
escapist magic of cinema. He loved how big, spectacular and
fantastical the film was and he had always tried to recreate
that childhood experience of watching The Spy Who Loved Me
in his own films.

(990) Skyfall's cast got through 200,000 rounds of
ammunition during their weapons training.

(991) Terence Young felt that Thunderball was the movie where fantasy and gadgetry got out of hand and they started to repeat themselves. It probably explains why never directed another Bond movie after Thunderball.

(992) Cubby Broccoli apparently cast Britt Ekland in The Man With the Golden Gun after being impressed by her nude scene in the classic British folk horror The Wicker Man. What Cubby didn't know was that Ekland had a body double on The Wicker Man. That wasn't really her bottom in the film.

(993) The voice of Draco in On Her Majesty's Secret Service was dubbed by David de Keyser.

(994) you could argue that Roger Moore's finest hour as Bond comes in Moonraker when Bond emerges from the centrifuge and looks genuinely rattled. To achieve the rippled effect on Bond's face from the G-forces, high-pressure hoses were rigged to blow at Roger's face.

(995) The crew on The Spy Who Loved Me nicknamed the underwater Lotus 'Wet Nellie' in tribute to little Nellie from You Only Live Twice.

(996) Kim Basinger had to wear a wig on Never Say Never Again reshoots because she'd already cut her cut for another film.

(997) Barbara Carrera is the only actress to be nominated for portraying a Bond Girl at the Golden Globes. It must have really annoyed EON that this moment of Bond history came in an unofficial Bond film!

(998) The Man with the Golden Gun was known as 007 Against The Man With The Golden Pistol in Brazil.

(999) A 37 page story treatment for Timothy Dalton's (ultimately doomed) third Bond film titled Reunion in Death was delivered by Richard Smith near the end of 1993. Reunion

in Death was heavily inspired by the Ian Fleming novel You Only Live Twice. Fleming's You Only Live Twice takes place after the shattering events of On Her Majesty's Secret Service. The story in Richard Smith's Reunion in Death has Bond in Japan investigating Yasuhiro Nakasone - an industrialist connected to the Yakuza. Nakasone's wife Michiko serves as one of Bond's allies though. The plot of Reunion with Death revolves around the murder of Sir Robert Grey - a friend of M. It was of course Nakasone who was behind the murder because of his desire to control the world's microchip market. Interestingly, Bond's secretary Loelia Ponsonby is a character in Reunion in Death. The treatment begins with Bond killing an agent in a skyscraper. The skyscraper PTS in Reunion in Death ends with Bond parachuting from the building.

(1000) The Living Daylights was called Icecold Mission in Sweden.